Pet Parents

Pet Parents

A Journey Through Unconditional Love and Grief

BY COLEEN ELLIS

WITH A FOREWORD BY DR. MARTY BECKER
AMERICA'S VETERINARIAN

iUniverse, Inc.
Bloomington

Pet Parents
A Journey Through Unconditional Love and Grief

iUniverse books may be ordered through booksellers or by contacting:

iUniverse
1663 Liberty Drive
Bloomington, IN 47403
www.iuniverse.com
1-800-Authors (1-800-288-4677)

ISBN: 978-1-4620-3548-9 (sc)
ISBN: 978-1-4620-3549-6 (ebk)

Printed in the United States of America

iUniverse rev. date: 02/16/2012

CONTENTS

FOREWORD

By Dr. Marty Becker
"America's Veterinarian"

As a veterinarian, I focus on keeping pets alive. It's something I'm good at, and I enjoy sharing my expertise with others to help them keep their pets healthy and happy.

It's always a thrill for me to help someone with the tips I share on "Good Morning America" and "The Dr. Oz Show." I've also been blessed to serve as the pet expert for the American Association of Retired Persons, and I'm also the veterinary spokesman for top animal health companies. I also operate www.petconnection.com with Gina Spadafori, who has been writing about pets for almost thirty years. My books, such as "Your Dog: The Owner's Manual", "The Ultimate Dog Lover", "The Ultimate Cat Lover", and others have helped people throughout the world celebrate their special bond with their pets. You can learn more about all that I do on my website.

But no matter how much we love and take care of our pets, they do eventually die. As a veterinarian, I've always been sympathetic to this fact, but it wasn't until I spoke as a keynote speaker at the Pet Loss Professionals Alliance convention that I realized that there are so many options out there for a pet parent who wants to honor the life of a beloved pet upon death.

At the PLPA convention, which is part of the larger International Cemetery, Cremation and Funeral Association, I was pleased to reconnect with Coleen Ellis. I met Coleen many years ago on a speaking trip to Indianapolis where I first learned about her stand-alone pet funeral home, the first of its kind in the United States. I'm pleased that she's now a part of Two Hearts Pet Loss Center, which serves as a resource to help professionals help bereaved pet owners. She's also the co-chairperson at the PLPA and is as passionate about helping pet parents as I am about helping animals. She has a contagious love for animals, which I can definitely appreciate.

Speaking to Coleen those many years ago, I learned about her heartbreaking story of losing her dog Mico. She wanted to mourn her loss just as she would have mourned the loss of a human family member, but no one was there to help her do this. Coleen knew that she wasn't alone, and she took courageous action to ensure that the next time someone in her community lost a pet, they would have more options. This is a mission that Coleen continues to this day, and you can tell how passionate she is about helping pet parents as soon as you meet her.

But this isn't just Coleen's story. This book is the story of pet parents throughout the United States and beyond. It's the story of how people are dealing with the profound loss of their beloved pets and a story that shows all pet owners who are having a hard time dealing with loss that they are not alone.

It's also the story of veterinarians who must try to navigate a new world where people have deeper connections with their pets than ever. It can be difficult for veterinarians to transition to helping pet parents who suffer the loss of a pet when we are rightly focused on saving and improving their lives. Fortunately, there are pet loss professionals to help pet parents deal with these issues and to hold ceremonies to honor the special bonds that owners have with their pets.

It may surprise some people to know, but in addition to there being pet loss professionals that help pet parents memorialize pets, there is also a growing contingent of funeral homes that are beginning to cater to pet parents. Coleen does a great job explaining the services out there, and the information she shares will help pet owners decide what's best for them and why.

Also, just as there are options to help people remember their human family members, people want to remember their pets as well. It can be helpful and meaningful to purchase something that honors the special relationship you had with your pet as well as to let others know how much you are hurting. It could be a necklace with a photo of your dog or cat, a special urn to hold your pet's cremated remains or a portrait of your pet. Sadly, pet parents don't know what they don't know. Luckily, Coleen's book equips pet parents with knowledge and solutions.

There are some great things going on in the field of pet loss and pet memorialization, but like any business, there are unscrupulous operators. These are the people who will push you when you are down or refuse to answer your questions. There are businesses that will not treat your pet's remains in the way you deem dignified. Coleen helps you ask the right questions to ensure that your pet is cared for properly.

Coleen is doing some tremendous things when it comes to helping pet parents grieve and remember their pets. As a veterinarian, I know firsthand that pet owners can feel a tremendous loss when they lose a pet – sometimes this loss is just as profound if not more so than when they lose a human family member.

I'm happy to have met Coleen, and this book helped me develop a better understanding of what pet parents want when they lose a pet and how to meet those needs. I think it's an important resource for any pet parent who anticipates losing a beloved pet or who wants to know that they are not alone in wanting options. It's also an important book for veterinarians, grief professionals and anyone who has someone important in their life who is a pet parent.

ACKNOWLEDGEMENTS

With my deepest gratitude, I thank my dear friend and colleague, Thomas A. Parmalee, for making this project possible. Without his guidance and writing talent, the words would not have danced like he made them dance.

To my many professional colleagues who elevated this topic of respectful pet loss services, without your voices, my voice would not have been as powerful.

For my Mom, the one who taught my brothers and me the special love of an animal. She always allowed the strays to stay and encouraged my passion for our furry friends.

And, for my daily support, the one who has encouraged me, inspired me and has been my cheerleader, my husband, Chris Burke. Without your insight, your guidance, and your support, my passion would not have happened. I will be eternally grateful.

I also want to thank my children, Brian and Amy. Brian, for being with me at the start of this journey and believing in the mission. Your hard work was amazing. Amy, for your love for the animals.

But, most of all, my thanks to those that have shaped this message – my beloved pets. With you, I learned life's lessons of forgiveness, how to live in the moment and see its beauty, but most of all, I learned unconditional love. All my love to Mike the Dog, Crisco, Ellie Mae, and Rudy.

Lastly, my biggest thanks to Mico – pictured with me on the next page – Mommy's Baby Girl, for starting this journey that I now humbly walk with others.

Coleen & Mico

CHAPTER 1

My Story

Here I am with Mico.

It was the day after Easter, 2003. It had been a long eight months for my little terrier-schnauzer mix, my little baby girl, Mico. The ugliness of the lung cancer had taken its toll on her little body. Nevertheless, in true form to her feistiness and spirit—she held on until the very last minute.

As I watched her on the operating table, I recalled picking her out 14 years ago at the Humane Society in Wichita, Kan. I had just moved into my first home, and I was ready to get a furry little child. Growing up with pets, I knew that no home was complete without animals. Mom made sure that we had our fair share of fur love, and there was a constant parade of beautiful creatures walking through our doors. Blackie, Buddy, Snobal, Sparky, Frisky 1, Frisky 2, Frisky 3 (we couldn't seem to get creative on the names for our cats), Fred – the list goes on and on.

When I walked through the Humane Society's doors on a beautiful Sunday afternoon in 1989, I saw all 2 pounds of Mico. She was sharing a newspaper-lined fish aquarium with a not-so-feisty baby Doberman. She **demanded** attention, and she was going to get it. I immediately fell head over heels in love. I am still not sure if I gave her my heart or if she just stole it, but it was all hers!

She came home and immediately ruled the house. But what was even more interesting was how she commanded a presence wherever she went. She walked into life and each situation as if it were already hers. In reality, she never really walked into anything. *She ran!* She always wanted to be in the middle of everything. It was as if every circumstance was a beautiful adventure, just waiting for her to get involved. She would look at each encounter as if it were the most incredible event that held such wonder. Her eyes always seemed to say, "Mommy, look at this beautiful thing called life that we are sharing together." Whether it was her surroundings or the new friends she was about to meet, it was all so magnificent! Her confidence, lack of fear, and enthusiasm for everything was so much fun to watch. Even if I didn't know it at the time, I knew that she was teaching me how to live life.

But as I remembered all our good times, she was on the operating table. The doctor summoned me to come in and say goodbye, and it was clear that she was not going to wake up after the surgery. How do you sum up 14 years in just a few minutes?

How do I tell her what she's meant to me?
How do I thank her for what she's done for me?
How do I let her know that I will ALWAYS love her?
How?

"I love you" seemed so small, but that's all I could say. But I said it, and over and over again. I was just hoping that it summed it all up for her, too. In a minute, it was all over. My precious little girl was gone.

A Lack of Options

With that, we had to move forward with the final arrangements for her precious little body. Unfortunately, the choices presented to us were not what I wanted for my special little girl. As I considered these death-care options that seemed disrespectful, my heart started to break into a million pieces. She deserved so much more in this area of finality. I did not want her to be treated like an animal. I wanted her to be treated like a special little member of the family. But without any other recourse, we made her final arrangements, even though they fell far short from what she deserved.

It didn't seem right to me, and it was at that moment that I made my vow. No pet parent should have to be put in the position of "disposing" of their pet when they really want to honor them and their remains with a meaningful ceremony. I made a vow that I would change how this process is done and that pet parents would have the options they wanted and needed to truly pay tribute to their precious little pets.

I wanted there to be a place that would guide people and help them through the wilderness of incredible grief that becomes apparent when a loved pet dies. I thought back to what I would have done to have properly honored Mico, and I knew that many others just like me wanted the opportunity to say and feel that special goodbye that I never was given.

The Beginning of My Mission

When I watched little Mico die, the idea for the first standalone pet funeral home in the United States was conceived. Months later, I opened the doors to Pet Angel Memorial Center. I wanted each pet to be given the dignity and respect in death that they so deserved. And just as importantly, we would help pet parents through the difficult journey.

The Pet Angel Memorial Center provided a place for pet parents to say goodbye to their pets in a way that fit into their normal family rituals. It gave them a safe place to mourn and cry without judgment, and they felt the love as soon as they walked in the front door. We educated families about all of their options, and served as a companion for families that needed one. These were the things I wanted when I lost my little Mico.

My husband, Chris Burke, joined me in starting the business, and he was a natural as a business partner. As a pet lover himself, he played a critical role behind the scenes and helped to manage the operation. He was also there at my side as I helped families deal with their loss and participated at pet fairs and rescue events. We both brought our individual and unique talents to Pet Angel, pulling it all together under the umbrella of one common mission: to make sure that each pet was given the dignity and respect that they deserved in death.

I was also blessed to have my stepson, Brian, join the business, too. For a young man, this opportunity of being with me in this type of start-up business was very exciting for him. To this day, I'm amazed at the compassion and care that Brian has for all of the families that he works with. He is an old soul in a very mature young man's body, and he has made an impression on countless families in the Indianapolis area where Pet Angel began. I was proud that he wanted to join me in helping families.

While my work as a pet funeral director was not physically challenging, I ended each day emotionally exhausted. Families looked to me and my team as they tried to make sense of their feelings. So many of them had been told that they should not feel so torn up over the loss of a pet, but we were there to tell them differently. Our message and personal service set us apart, and we truly became the place where pet parents turned to upon losing a special family friend. We made sure that the value of the service clearly outweighed the price that was paid, making sure that each family received 110 percent.

As my work at Pet Angel grew, my world started to become even bigger. People, organizations, and existing businesses all over the world wanted to know about my mission and whether or not people really saw value in what I was doing. *Did people really want to do all of these things for just a dog? For just a cat? And what about the more unusual pets, like lizards, pigs and horses?*

Most of the people who initially contacted me were under the impression that the pet parents who wanted to do these things were eccentric or people who had no friends other than their pets. But they soon came to realize that everyday people really want to honor their pets, and the interest in what I was doing exploded. It became clear that people are hungry for the permission to honor their furry children. They desperately want someone to validate their feelings over losing a precious member of the family. Part of it was about having more options. But they also want and need a place to go to for emotional support. Yes, that's what it is truly all about.

With so many people intrigued by my business concept, I spread my wings even further and launched Two Hearts Pet Loss Center. Two Hearts is here to guide those who also want to help their communities pay tribute to beloved pets. For funeral homes, it's the opportunity to fully serve the entire family. For other organizations, it provides an outlet to give pets the dignity and respect they deserve, in life and in death.

It is an interesting life calling. While many people don't understand the human-animal companion bond, these are the same people who don't understand the grief that comes with the death of a beloved pet. But for so many of us, this ordeal can be just as painful if not *more* painful than losing a human friend or family member. While there are no possessions to divide and no reading of wills, dealing with a loss of a pet can be emotional and complicated.

Spreading the Word

When the Pet Angel story began to hit the news, the funeral industry in particular was completely intrigued by this concept. A small number of funeral homes already helped people deal with the loss of a pet family member as a smaller component of their larger business, but our story helped other mortuaries see that this was another way they could help families.

I began speaking at conventions that serve the funeral profession, such as the National Funeral Directors Association, the International Cemetery, Crematory and Funeral Association and other death-care groups. It was during these conferences that I first got to know a number of journalists at death care publications. Journalists such as Tom Parmalee with Kates-Boylston Publications and Susan Loving, editor of the International Cemetery, Cremation and Funeral Association's magazine, helped spread the word about what I was doing and why it is important.

In my travels, I met so many people who shared my belief that pets are essential members of the family and that owners should be given options to grieve when their pets die. Unfortunately, for too long, pet parents have felt that they shouldn't feel so bad when a pet dies. They haven't known about all the options they have when it comes to honoring and paying tribute to a beloved pet family member. And they haven't been told that there are so many others out there just like them. I wrote this book to tell you about your choices, to share with the world the stories of others who have gone through this ordeal in a more meaningful way and to help all the pet parents who don't think they have options to deal with their loss in ways that honor their beloved pets.

CHAPTER 2

The Role of Professionals in the Loss of a Pet

The families in Ormond Beach, Fla., are blessed to have caring professionals like the Lohman Family, who operate Lohman Funeral Homes, to help them when their precious pets die. In the picture above, Nancy Lohman honors her beautiful cat, Stretch, in a memorial service that paid tribute to the love that they all shared together.

I still remember how empty I felt at the veterinarian's office when I lost Mico. When the veterinarian told me the options that were available to me as far as "disposing" of her remains, I was so upset. I wanted to pay tribute to Mico and honor her in a way that fit the special bond we shared.

I also remember how I felt when I went to the human funeral home that ultimately ended up being the operation that performed her cremation. When we arrived at the funeral home with her deceased body, Chris and I asked if we could sit in the chapel with her for a few more precious minutes. The staff there told me that I could, however, they also requested that I sit in the back of the chapel and not turn the lights on as they had a family in their funeral home with a "real death." They, too, minimized my feelings of loss and grief – because it was "just a dog."

After starting Pet Angel and now as the operator of Two Hearts Pet Loss Center, I know that I'm not the only one who feels that the veterinarian community can do better. They do a tremendous job in keeping our loved animals alive, but all too often, they just don't know how to handle the death of a beloved pet. Thankfully, this is changing, *but pet parents want it to change faster!* I know with continued education of other pet care professionals, pet parents will be given every option that they need to honor the life that they shared with their special pets. This should come from all pet care professionals – in the veterinary world as well as in the death-care industry.

Debbie Lucas, a 57-year-old nurse, whose dog Moet died at age 15, feels similar to many of the clients I have served. "At about age 13, Moet developed bladder cancer, and I remember asking my veterinarian what death-care options were available," she told me. "And I was basically given a brochure of a company out of Fort Wayne, Ind., and told that they traveled around to veterinarian offices to pick up and cremate bodies." She added, "I had a couple options: Moet could be cremated in a group with no ashes returned or cremated privately and I'd get her ashes back. But I wasn't really happy with that option as I didn't know if I'd really be getting **her** ashes."

Debbie came to me after calling a grief counselor who knew about what I did at Pet Angel. With me, she found an option that allowed her to pay respect to not only Moet's body but to pay tribute to the life and the memories they shared. I was going to make sure that Moet's body was not shipped away impersonally in a truck with the bodies of so many other pets.

I also helped Shawn and Steve Cardwell, who needed me to take care of their dog Squirty. "Basically, I have both good and bad feelings about the veterinarian," Steve would tell me later. "We took him to the vet when we noticed symptoms, and they were the ones who found the cancer. But then we went back toward the end of his life (after taking him to a hospital for chemotherapy for a stretch of time) and – the night he died specifically – they had some woman on duty who we had never worked with before. She was sweet and kind, but she was detached." He added, "It was tough to walk away from that room leaving Squirty right there on the table. When I recollect it, I think they could have been . . . well, you are talking to people who are not thinking clearly and maybe they could have given us more direction."

Scott Emch, a veterinarian who operates Well Pets Economy Clinics, a mobile veterinary clinic business that operates throughout central Indiana, regularly works with bereaved pet owners. Over the past couple of years, he has increasingly been visiting pet parents at their own homes to respectfully euthanize their loved pets. He partly attributes the increasing popularity of this new service to the way pet parents feel when they go to veterinarian offices to euthanize their pets. "I started doing this a little bit here and there for some friends, and the response I got from people was so incredibly positive," he said. "To be able to do this quietly and peacefully is great (for pet parents)."

Emch has been in practice for 20 years, and he says that veterinarians in general need to improve how they handle the deaths of pets. "I think as long as there have been small animal veterinarians, euthanasia has been part of that equation, and the care and tenderness and appropriateness of how it was done would vary with the veterinarian," he said. "Some veterinarians have a very utilitarian view of animals, and there may be some people who are not as compassionate. But other veterinarians are very good with people."

Fortunately, veterinarians have begun to change over the past 10 to 15 years as society as a whole has begun to appreciate the strong bond that can exist between humans and animals. "Sometimes, people would say, 'it's just a pet; can't you just get over it?' And they didn't understand it is like a family member, and the loss of what someone experiences can be very similar to losing a brother, spouse or child," Emch said. "So the whole field of catering to that and realizing how deep that bond goes with certain people means that there is more emphasis on things like written materials and support groups. Now, some veterinarian hospitals have special rooms dedicated to euthanasia."

As a pet parent, and as a pet loss professional, I'm proud to lead the educational charge on the fact that pet parents *do* want more. We ask for more in the medical treatment of our pets in life – and we are going to ask for more in the options that we have available to us when our beloved pets die. For you, the pet parent, it is your responsibility to ask questions about your options for medical care and to fully understand what happens when your pet dies. Be informed!

Veterinarians Lose Pets, Too

While some veterinarians might seem cold and impersonal in the loss of a pet, the vast majority really do the best they can for the families they serve, given the minimal amount of grief and loss training that they get on this subject in their educational studies.

Let's remember, however, that the vast majority of veterinarians went into the business because they love animals. And many of them have pets of their own and sometimes discover for the first time how devastated their clients can feel when they lose a pet of their own.

Later, I'll share the story of Shelly Zacharias, a wonderful veterinarian who has lost many pets of her own. Shelly recently shared her home with nine dogs, nine cats, three rabbits and a guinea pig. Emily, her Border collie mix, is a therapy dog who accompanies her to elementary schools. She enjoys educating children about basic animal welfare. When it comes to helping pet parents deal with the loss of a beloved pet, she truly cares about helping her clients.

Shelly has been in the veterinary field for 20 years and graduated in 2004 from Oklahoma State. "There, they had an ethics class where they touched on euthanasia and grieving, but when they talked about euthanasia, it focused more on how not to offend the owner," she said. "I do think helping pet owners through the grieving process is starting to become more recognized, but I also think it is starting to become more of a business. Veterinarians and institutions are starting to realize not just the emotional reasons for it but also that this is a way to make money. So they are paying more attention to it."

Like me, Shelly focuses on this area because she sees it as an emotional issue and believes that pets need to be respected. Others in the field obviously feel the same. "Ten years ago, whenever I'd go to national meetings, there was never a topic about this on the agenda," she said. "But now when I go to national meetings, the topic of grief is always covered. I think this is a good thing."

Sadly, there are still veterinarians who work mainly with waste disposers that basically throw out the bodies of pets with the trash. Many times, pet parents do not know what is happening with their pets. "I think this is very disrespectful, and there are still clinics that do that," Shelly said. "I think maybe the public is just naïve and doesn't ask for details. But many people do care about what happens to their pets. They just can't fathom that they are not going to be taken care of in this regard, and they think they will be taken care of more respectfully than just being part of the garbage."

Veterinarians in Shelly's area use a service where when pets are cremated as part of a group, their remains are properly disposed of in a dignified way, which is clearly much better than disposal-type services. "We keep fliers out all the time about the different options out there, and whenever we have someone who has had a pet pass away or we know it is going to be euthanized, I am the one who talks to them specifically about their options," she said.

In most cases, pet parents who have to euthanize their pets have a harder time dealing with the loss than a pet that dies naturally. "People are relieved that a pet has passed away in their bed or at home," she said. "More people seem to struggle in having to bring in a pet for euthanasia because then they have to be actively involved in the process."

While I was the first person to open a standalone pet funeral home in the United States, others have now begun to offer this service, and it's something I couldn't be happier about. Human funeral homes are also increasingly getting involved in offering pet cremation and memorial options. When I asked Shelly what she thought about this, she said, "It's about time!" She added, "But this is one area where I think they are getting involved because of the financial part of it, but hopefully some of them are doing it because they think it's time that pets be respected in that way."

Working with families with beloved pets that are dying is still a "work in progress" within the veterinary industry, Shelly said. "While I like to put the family at ease when they have a pet that is dying or has died, I know that our industry has some work to do with this," she said. "What I would like to see is my colleagues getting better about talking to people about what to do with their pets after they pass away and some of the options they have and the different ways to respect them after they are gone. There are many ways to remember them."

There are benefits to honoring pets in the proper way, Shelly believes. "I think if we respect them more after they pass, it will help people think of them more as part of the family when they are alive," she said. "And if we can get people to treat pets more as members of the family, that will help make the lives of pets better."

Change Continues

Pet Angel and Two Hearts Pet Loss Center have educated a lot of people in the Indianapolis area and beyond about how people can pay tribute to their pets, but I want everyone everywhere to realize that they are not alone in wanting to honor the life stories of their pets.

This aspiration is starting to take hold, according to Theresa Huber, practice manager at the Bargersville Veterinary Hospital & Wellness Center in Franklin, Ind. "Even before you started Pet Angel, people were starting to request private cremations more than they had been," Theresa told me. "And now they seem a bit more concerned about getting their pets back, the cremation and having an urn."

In large part, this is due to the overall shift of how society looks at pets. "They have gone from being farm dogs to a lot of people to being their kids," Theresa said. "So they are more of a family member than a farm implement."

It is hard for veterinarians to always know what a pet parent is going through, which is one of the reasons why it's great that pet bereavement specialists are now offering services, Theresa said. "For one, we don't have the training, and two, one only has so much time," she said. "It's nice to have services like this so that for that person who calls us and says, 'I'm having a horrible day; everything I see reminds me of Fluffy' – now there is someone to talk to about that."

Of course, there are still some clients who come in with a dog that they look at as "just a dog." Theresa understands how the more emotionally involved people feel, however, because when she lost her dog Zeus at age 6 from cancer, she came to me for help. "It's always different when it's your own," Theresa said.

Now, when a client is having a hard time dealing with the loss of a pet, Theresa will share her own experience. "Usually we present brochures, and I can try to see what it is they need," she said. "They may be someone who wants a memorial, someone who wants an urn or someone who wants everything – an urn, a blanket done with the pet's picture, nose prints. It's about trying to feel out the client."

Another friend and colleague of mine, Brenda Tassava, a certified veterinary practice manager and the hospital administrator at Broad Ripple Animal Clinic in Indianapolis, knows that her clients are seeking more in terms of after-death care and support after the loss of a pet. I've worked with them regularly to provide the level of service, support and guidance that they need in working with clients.

Overall, Brenda sees that veterinary practices have taken a wide variety of approaches to how they handle the loss of pets. "Many things have evolved, but it remains one of the most difficult things we deal with on a daily basis," she said. "The nature of veterinary care is to heal the pet and foster the human-animal bond. Animal caregivers in the veterinary field experience grief every day when we have to euthanize a pet. This is probably the one area of medicine that is very different when you compare human medicine to veterinary medicine." She added, "We have evolved a great deal in the past 15 to 20 years. As examples: Some practices employ the use of a 'comfort room' used strictly for euthanasia and/or ICU visitation; many practices make clay paw prints to mail to clients with a sympathy card following the loss of a pet; practices without comfort rooms may denote the exam room number in the record where a client experienced the loss of a pet in an effort not to seat them in that same room with future pets."

It's clear that clients are changing, however, and about 40 percent of pet parents at Broad Ripple want a private cremation with the remains of their pet returned to them. Still, Brenda thinks that more support for the veterinarian community is needed. "We don't have enough training or resources available to us to improve skills in this area," she said. "Continuing education for veterinarians addresses advances in medical procedures, treatments, etc. There is a need for improving our sensitivity and approach as well as grief support for our staff."

The bottom line is that veterinarians need to better equip themselves to handle grief in order to help their families, Brenda said. "They also need to be able to support their employees and staff when they go through the emotional roller coaster of assisting in euthanasia then immediately needing to shift gears to do a new puppy appointment."

In the following chapters, I'll show you firsthand how an increasing number of pet parents are dealing with loss in a more meaningful way, and I'll also take the initial steps needed to help pet care professionals understand some of the many issues their clients deal with and how they can help them with a healthy grief journey through an active mourning process.

Pet parents don't know what they don't know, but the following stories will show the many options and possibilities that are available. From one pet parent to another, I think that you will find some peace in knowing that you are not alone and that there are options for you and your family in honoring the life that you shared with your precious pet.

A Letter from Coleen Ellis to the Veterinarian Community

Dear Pet Care Professional:

In your industry of pet care, there has been an ever-changing world in health practices. You've also faced new and changing demands from pet parents. I applaud you for keeping up with these continuous changes and for making sure that my precious little pet, that all precious little pets, are getting only the best of care.

With this book, I come to you with a request that comes from me in my role as a pet loss professional and also as a pet parent. Throughout the lifetime that every pet parent will share with their pet, you will see us through the baby stages and many times on into the geriatric days. The years will fly by way too fast – and before we know it we will be having some difficult conversations, and ultimately decisions, regarding the final days of our pet's life.

As the final days approach in the life of a pet, you will have the same discussions that you have had with countless other pet parents. This time of talking about palliative care or even possibly euthanasia may be conversations that are a part of your day-to-day work regime. But it will be the first time that many of your clients have had to talk about these matters. And, if it's not the first time, it's still LIKE the first time. Every time it will be like the first time.

My plea to you: Please realize that many of your clients view their pet as a precious, beloved child. We know that you did everything you could for our special little pets in life, but now we need to know that you will be doing everything that you can to guide us after our pet's death.

We might need things that would be considered "out of the norm" in your world, but in all actuality, they will be things that we will want to do to pay tribute to a beloved pet. Don't judge us for what we need, and don't assume that you will know what your clients will need. Find those resources that will be able to guide us, to let us honor our stories, and to do what we need to do as that one last thing. We need someone that will have the skills to walk us through this process. Someone that can tenderly guide us in an area in which we don't know what we don't know.

*But it's even more than that. For many pet parents, this time of death is a time in which we feel incredibly alone. Our circle of friends may not have understood the special life that we shared with a pet, and they probably won't understand the loneliness and grief we suffer when a pet dies. I as a grieving pet parent will want support during this time – I will **need** that support. I will want someone to companion me through this time as the darkness of night will be overwhelming. Please help me and every other pet parent honor our pets and the times that we shared with them.*

As pet parents, this is the least we can do. We WANT to do this.

As a pet loss professional, I can assure you that pet parents just do not know the various options available to honor their pets in death. Don't short-change them because you are pressed for time or don't think this is important. So many times I have had pet parents say to me, "I wish I would've known about THAT because I would've loved to have done it." We are professionals, and it is our responsibility to educate these grieving pet parents on what their options are, leaving them to choose for themselves what is important. Don't deny them those opportunities for choices.

In advance, on behalf of all pet parents, I thank you. I thank you for caring about my precious little pet and every other pet out there – and also for caring about me and my needs and wants.

Warm Regards,
Coleen Ellis

CHAPTER 3

This Veterinarian's Pets are her Career and Family, Too

Just as some veterinarians can do a better job serving pet parents, there are others who know firsthand how hard it is to lose a beloved pet. These veterinarians are often the same ones who are willing to provide pet parents with the information they need to grieve and deal with such a tremendous loss. These are veterinarians like Dr. Shelly Zacharias.

I knew the minute I met Shelly that she was special. She loved her pets so much that they had shaped her world and had led her to become a veterinarian. She loved her pet children, she loved her animal patients and she cared for the owners who came to her seeking help.

She gave all she could to each of those aspects of her life. Therefore, when it came time to help her with the little pets that started her life's career journey, I knew that it was going to be an incredibly deep and emotional journey. Not only for her but for those around her who loved her, too.

Shelly knew that Macy, her little dog, would die soon from cancer. But just as she was preparing herself for this loss, her 21-year-old cat, Caddy Jo, died.

"Caddy was normal one day, and I came home and she was just lying on the floor," Shelly said. "I had to take her to emergency surgery and they found that she was full of cancer. She was euthanized right on the table. It all happened in a six-hour period, and it was a complete surprise."

With Macy, she was at least prepared for what was to come. That didn't make it much easier, however, as she shared an even stronger and more special bond with her dog. Shelly's former practice was named "Macy's Veterinary Hospital," and Macy joined her every day at the office.

"People knew that I named the practice after her and how much she meant to me," Shelly said. "She was like my child."

People kept telling Shelly that it was time to euthanize Macy. "I knew it was getting close," she said. "She had been having chemotherapy for nine months, and I knew that it was getting to the point that it was more for me," she said.

Three days later, she had Macy euthanized.

Mixed Emotions

I now had both Caddy Jo and Macy at my memorial center. Both of their beautiful bodies were waiting for Shelly when she came in for her first visitation.

For a few days, Shelly continued to visit both of her pets as they peacefully rested. "I just can't let them go," she told me. This continued until I suggested that we have a little ceremony to help her say goodbye.

Recalling the experience later, Shelly told me, "I wasn't completely on board. I really didn't know how I felt about it, but I really didn't have to do anything except show up." We put together a handout that had both Caddy Jo's picture and Macy's picture. Shelly wrote eulogies for each of them. And many of Shelly's clients who knew her pets attended the service.

The support from her local friends and clients was important and meant a lot. As a single pet parent mom with no human children, Shelly's entire family also treasured Macy. They had flown in from Oklahoma to visit her when Macy was going through chemotherapy, but they couldn't be there for the remembrance ceremony.

In preparing for the service, it was essential that each detail was handled with the dignity and grace that it needed. I knew that there would be numerous people in attendance, and I wanted to make sure that for Shelly, this memorial event was all Macy and Caddy Jo deserved. And, truthfully, I wanted it to be absolutely incredible as it's what Shelly deserved, too, as she honored these precious loves in her life.

We prepared their bodies to lay side-by-side, in state. They were absolutely beautiful. When people arrived at the service, they were given a service card and then escorted to the front of the chapel to pay their respects – and to share their love with Shelly. The emotions were high, and the room was full of love.

The formal service was standing-room only. We had a register book where everyone signed their name. The service started with a prayer, bringing everyone in attendance to one reverent mind as we prepared to honor these two beautiful pets. Another practice that I like to do to start services, and this one was no different, was the lighting of the candle and the reading of the poem, "In the Candle's Glow," by Laura Hickman. It truly speaks to the fact that our pet friends are looking down on us – as we turn to the glow of a candle for comfort, warmth and reflection. The lighting of the candle was especially moving as Shelly lit two candles. All I could think of was how her heart must be in pieces.

Later, Shelly shared a story about each of her pets. As she spoke about each of them, I stood beside her to help her get through each story. As she talked, Macy and Caddy Jo were behind us in their little caskets. There were tears, there was laughter and there was love.

To end this most beautiful service, Shelly wanted to give a toast honoring Macy and Caddy Jo. But it wasn't just any toast! The toast had to be fitting – it had to be perfect. Therefore, as I listened to Shelly in how we were going to honor these loves, she made mention of a game that her and Macy would play. It was a game where Shelly would cover her eyes and play a version of a peek-a-boo game. Therefore, to end the service, each attendee received a glass of wine, and Shelly covered her eyes, threw her hand off of her face and gave her final farewell and send-off to Macy and Caddy Jo. There was not a dry eye in the room, and it was incredibly touching. Even more touching was how Shelly's friends and pet parent clients stayed throughout the service to be with Shelly, Macy and Caddy Jo. It was about 10:30 p.m. before everyone started making their way home.

Reflecting on a Powerful Event

"By the time it was over, I felt complete and as though something had been done for them," Shelley said later. "I felt like I could let them go; it really made a big difference in the way I felt because it seemed like everything was OK." She added, "It was probably one of the most heartfelt experiences I had in my entire life."

Each of her pets was cremated, and the next day, she had them in their urns. "I chose to have the ashes back instead of having them scattered," Shelley said. "I picked out a special urn for each of their personalities. For instance, Macy was a little princess, so I picked out a little pink, flower urn because it fit her personality perfectly."

Shelly was grateful that a couple that she is good friends with paid for the funeral, and she picked out and paid for each urn along with necklaces and bracelets that have lockets containing a portion of cremated remains from each pet. "Since then, I've lost several pets, and for every pet I buy a piece of jewelry that I wear with the ashes," she said. Since Macy died, she has never taken off the necklace she wears honoring the special bond that they share.

"If I have a date or a friend, and I tell them about what I did for Macy or for one of my pets, no one has really come back and said anything rude because I tend to get emotional, and they know what I do for a living," she said. Still, she knows that some people may think honoring her pets in such a way is unusual. "But so far, no one has said anything to me offensive," she said.

A Letter to All Pet Parents

My Dear Pet Parent:

Even though Shelly was at first unsure if she should hold a service, she has no regrets. "It really changed the way I felt about being able to let them go," she said. "I recommend services for pets all the time now. I was never against it, but when I lost my pets, I was just so hurt. I didn't want to see anyone at that time, but this made me feel better, happier and it felt good to talk about Macy and how much she meant to me."

I have told countless families that having a memorial service or funeral service for our pets is a natural part of our society and rituals. We hold rituals for many other events, such as birthdays and holidays. Holding a ceremony for a beloved pet is only natural.

Shelly was like many people that I work with – she had a concern of what people were going to think about "going to a funeral for an animal." What was it going to look like? Was it going to be weird? Who else goes to a funeral for an animal?

To many, the whole concept appears out of the ordinary or even odd. However, just like with the people who came to Shelly's service, I beam when people come up to me afterward and say how beautiful the service was – and how it was not at all like they thought it would be. In fact, many times I hear "I hope my service is this beautiful when I die."

As with others, I had told Shelly that the importance of having a ceremony for Macy and Caddy Jo was about honoring them. But it was also about giving people the opportunity to show Shelly how much they loved her and to show their support during a time of devastating loss. A ceremony is not just about coming to a funeral for a pet but more about coming together to support a grieving heart.

Shelly tends to have many pets, and she doesn't have a service for each and every one of them. As with most pet parents, there are those special pets that come into our lives, and into our hearts, that having a memorial service would be just the right way to pay tribute to a life that was lived and shared. Shelly is no different. Macy and Caddy Jo gave her the start in her career and were with her during her veterinary classes and her start as a young adult. While every pet is special, there are those that will not only be in our heart but will take a piece of our heart with them when they go. It's only fitting to have a fitting goodbye to these pet family members that make such a difference in our lives.

Having a service for Macy and Caddy Jo has enabled each of them to continue to help people because of what those who attended the service saw in the beauty of honoring a deceased pet. "Even though Macy is gone, she's still touching the lives of people and helping people through the relationships she created in life," Shelly said, adding that memorializing pets in death will help everyone appreciate them more and treat them better. "I think if we rightfully respect when they die, it will help people think of them more as part of the family when they are alive," she said.

Beautifully said, Shelly! Beautifully said!

Warm Regards,
Coleen

CHAPTER 4

Creating a Ritual Experience for Your Pet

For Cajun's Family, placing his favorite treat jar filled with seasonal flowers was the perfect way to honor him at his burial site in their yard. When Cajun was alive, as friends came to visit, his family would yell, "Cajun, your friends are here!" What better way is there to remember this love than with a bench for his loved ones to sit on as they remember the joy and love he brought to all of them? Of course, it's appropriate that it says, "Cajun, your friends are here."

The relationship you had with your pet is unique, and the rituals you will want to conduct to honor your relationship and the life you shared will also be unique. These rituals will be as individual as the personality of your pet, the activities your pet enjoyed and the special times you shared together.

For many people, having a funeral or memorial service for a pet is something they want to do, however, they don't know how to go about creating the service. Let me guide you with some elements and ideas that you and your family can incorporate into a service to pay tribute to your special friend.

Is it OK to Do This?

Many families that I have worked with who have lost a pet expressed a desire to have a funeral or ceremony. However, many people are unclear if this is "acceptable" to do. I can tell you without a doubt – it's absolutely acceptable to do. In fact, I give you permission to honor and pay tribute to your pet in the way that is best for you! Do what you need to do to honor their life. Many families enjoy dressing up their pets for Halloween, giving their pets Christmas presents and celebrating birthday parties. Therefore, it should not seem peculiar to participate in a ritual when a pet dies.

I'll never forget when WISH TV Channel 8 reporter, Dick Wolfsie, asked me an interesting question when I opened my pet funeral home in 2004: "How do you invite people to a funeral for a pet?" he asked. "Isn't that a weird question to ask and one that is probably going to be met with resistance and hesitancy?"

I'm sure that the reporter is not the only one who has had that thought cross their mind. Many people have never been to a pet funeral or memorial service, and not everyone knows how to approach it. However, much like the funeral for a beloved human family member, funerals for pets are most definitely for the living. Therefore, my answer to Dick and to anyone who would ponder this is, "The invitation to have someone come to a funeral for a pet is more about the support that the grieving heart needs at this time." For instance, when Mico died, if I were inviting someone to a service for her, my invitation would have sounded something like, "My friend, you know how much Mico meant to me. This Sunday I'm having a service for her, and I could really use your friendship and support right now. Would you be available to come to the pet funeral home at 2:00 in the afternoon to be with me as I honor my precious little girl?"

Now, doesn't that sound warm and inviting? If I asked that question of my friends, I would certainly hope that they respected me enough to be with me, to show me their love, and to *want* to be a part of the support system that I needed at this time. And, as I've told many people, if someone *does not* want to come and support you, their friend, at this time, it may be time to re-evaluate the friendship!

Options for Ceremonies and Rituals

Having a ceremony for your beloved pet can be done in many different ways. As with any ritual, the layout of the service and the elements that will be included will depend on what you and your pet liked to do and what was special in your day-to-day life that you shared. Some of the areas for you to consider are:

- Will you want to invite family and friends?
- Will the service be a formal service or one that is a bit more casual in nature?
- Will the service be held at your home, a favorite park, a pet funeral home, a cemetery or some other venue?
- Will there be readings? Poetry? Music? Candle-lighting?
- Will you want to collect items at the service to donate to an animal shelter or rescue organization?

I have heard so many different and unique ways that families have come together to honor a pet, from formal services to more laid-back gatherings. Following are a few stories about what people have done in the privacy of their own homes to celebrate the life that they shared with the pet:

- "Sparky loved to run! Being a Husky, it was so hard to keep him contained in the yard. When he would get out of the yard, it was an event to catch him, get him in the car, and bring him home! We'd see him on the side of the road, open the door and yell 'Sparky go home!' He'd take off even faster! That was part of the game, too. In his honor our entire family is getting into our separate cars, each with a bit of Sparky's ashes, and we'll sprinkle these ashes as we drive down that county road near our home. Of course we'll yell out our windows 'Sparky, go home!' Such a tribute to our little runner!"—*In Memory of Sparky by Jacquie and David Wall*

- "Abbey was one of the family. So, just like you do at a human funeral, we set up a table at home with all of Abbey's special toys, blankets and treats. As each of us thought of something that we wanted to include on the table, we put it there. By the end of the week – what a site! She was our girl! And, we wrapped the week up with a pizza party and told Abbey stories. We all laughed and cried. It was what she deserved!"

- "There was a special spot that Mr. B liked in the flower garden outside. Oh, the naps that he would take here! At his tribute, we all went to that spot, planted a flower and told a memory that we had of Mr. B. Being a typical cat, Mr. B liked it when it was ALL about him! This was a perfect way to pay honor to my little guy!"

So what are some things that you can do for a pet's memorial service?

Certainly do not hesitate to look to an individual or business certified in pet loss to guide you in your service. Much like a funeral director, a pet loss professional is there to make sure that your service is carried out the way you want. However, even more so, it's at a time like this that you need to sit back and let others help, and the creation and execution of a memorial event for your beloved pet is a key area in which someone can help.

While the options and possibilities are endless for what can be done at the memorial service for your pet, here are some ideas and poems to guide you as you plan a service:

- Consider having the service outside where your pet liked to be.
- Think of all of the people that have been touched by your pet's personality and invite them to come.
- Read Biblical passages that reference animals.
- Read special excerpts from books about the love of a pet.
- Read poetry about the special love shared with a pet.
- If your pet did volunteer work as a therapy dog, include those people whose lives were touched by your dog. If your pet did work in the schools, let the children know and have a service so that they might honor the work your pet did.
- Have everyone bring a memory of your pet to include in a memory book.
- Have the guests bring a donation item for a local shelter in honor of your pet.
- Put together a memorial CD with photos of your pet's life set to favorite music.
- Write a letter to your pet to read at the service.
- Write a letter about your pet to read at the service.
- Allow others at the service to recall their memories of your pet.
- Have everyone light a candle in honor of your pet when they arrive at the ceremony.
- Serve pet related food items for your human guests at the service such as hot dogs, corn dogs, pigs in the blanket, puppy chow snack food, pup-cakes, etc. Or if your pet's favorite food was from a local fast food place, serve that food! Many families I worked with said their pet's favorite food was chicken nuggets – order them by the dozens for your guests!
- Serve other treats for any four-legged friends attending.
- Have drinks available to conduct "a memory toast" to your special friend.
- Have a pet blanket at the service that everyone could sign in honor of your pet.
- Have your guests all plant a flower in a particular flower garden in memory of your pet. Possibly for a fall service, each guest could plant a tulip bulb to bloom in the spring. Other great flowers/bushes to plant are forget-me-not flowers or a bleeding heart bush. Mark the area with a special marker or rock with the pet's name on it.
- If you will be having a service, consider putting together a service folder like the ones you often get when attending a person's funeral service. The card would lay out the

service and let guests know what to expect during the ceremony. (I'll include some examples for you later to use as a template.)

- Create a tribute table at your ceremony for the guests to look at. The table would include items that were important to you and your pet. These items might be:
    - Their leash.
    - Their collar.
    - Favorite treats.
    - Favorite blanket or pillow.
    - Favorite clothes.
    - Special music.
    - Favorite toys.
    - Photos.
    - Awards.
    - Registration/adoption papers.
    - A DVD player – playing a DVD of the pet's life, including audio pieces that would have the pet's meow, bark, chirping, or other special sounds.

Readings for Your Pet's Service

There are many beautiful poems and readings that might be a part of your service. Here are a few for you to consider:

Lend Me a Pup

I will lend to you for awhile a puppy, God said,
For you to love him while he lives and to mourn for him when he is gone.
Maybe for twelve or fourteen years, or maybe for two or three.
But will you, till I call him back take care of him for me?

He'll bring his charms to gladden you and (should his stay be brief) you'll always have his memories
as solace for your grief.
I cannot promise that he will stay, since all from earth return,
But there are lessons taught below
I want this pup to learn.

I've looked the whole world over in search of teachers true
And from the folk that crowd life's land
I have chosen you.
Now will you give him all your love
Don't think the labor vain

Nor hate me when I come to take my pup back again.

I fancied that I heard them say
"Dear Lord Thy Will Be Done,"
For all the joys this pup will bring, the risk of grief you'll run.
Will you shelter him with tenderness
Will you love him while you may
And for the happiness you'll know forever grateful stay.

But should I call him back much sooner than you've planned
Please brave the bitter grief that comes and try to understand.
If, by your love, you've managed my wishes to achieve,
In memory of him that you've loved, cherish every moment with your faithful bundle, and know he
loved you too.

—Author Unknown

Rainbow Bridge

There is a bridge connecting heaven and Earth.

It is called the Rainbow Bridge because of its many colors. Just this side of the Rainbow Bridge is a
land of meadows, hills and valleys, all of it covered with lush green grass.

When a beloved pet dies, the pet goes to this lovely land. There is always food and water and warm
spring weather. There, the old and frail animals are young again. Those who are maimed are made
whole once more. They play all day with each other, content and comfortable.

There is only one thing missing. They are not with the special person who loved them on Earth. So
each day they run and play until the day comes when one suddenly stops playing and looks up! Then,
the nose twitches! The ears are up! The eyes are staring! You have been seen, and that one suddenly
runs from the group!

You take him or her in your arms and embrace. Your face is kissed again and again and again, and
you look once more into the eyes of your trusting pet.

Then, together, you cross the Rainbow Bridge, never again to be separated.

—Anonymous

A Tribute to a Best Friend

Sunlight streams through windowpane unto a spot on the floor . . . . then I remember, it's where you used to lie, but now you are no more.
Our feet walk down a hall of carpet, and muted echoes sound . . . . then I remember,
It's where your paws would joyously abound.
A voice is heard along the road, and up beyond the hill, then I remember it can't be yours . . . . your golden voice is still.
But I'll take that vacant spot of floor and empty muted hall and lay them with the absent voice and unused dish along the wall.
I'll wrap these treasured memorials in a blanket of my love and keep them for my best friend until we meet above.

—Author Unknown

Sample Service Card Layouts

To conclude this chapter, I'd like to share some examples of personalized service folders. These can be a wonderful thing to provide for your guests so everyone can remember your pet and know what made him or her so special. You might want to also consider mailing these out to those who were not able to make it to the service.

Always a free spirit...

Max
1991 - 2005

Coleen Ellis

Our Best Friends

From the moment that I saw you,
Somehow I knew you needed me.
Someone who'd love and protect you,
To show you what it meant to be free.

And as the years went by,
I knew I could always depend on you.
To share in the times that were happy,
Or be at my side if the day had been blue.

I can remember so many quiet evenings,
As I'd watch you curl up on your bed.
I had always thought I was your teacher,
But, it seems the lesson was mine instead.

I learned so many things from someone
who never spoke a word.
I learned to listen with my heart,
I learned that love is felt, not heard.

When the day came that you had to leave me,
I thought my heart would break in two.
But I would've never learned what
unconditional love meant,
If it weren't for the friend I found in you.

Lorrie Neal
2003

May they rest in Joyful Peace with the Lord in the Kennels of Heaven.

Sasha

In Loving Memory of

Sasha

Memorial Service
3:00 Thursday, November 30, 2006
Pet Angel Memorial Service

Welcome	Pet Angel
Lighting of the Candle	Jake
The Husky Kind	Jake
A Prayer for Animals	Robi
Weep Not for Me	Katherine
North of the Rainbow Bridge	Jo
A Final Toast & Tribute	Dr. Sarah Jarrell
A Message from your Pet Angel	Pet Angel
Benediction	Pet Angel

CHAPTER 5

What You Need to Know About Pet Cremation

While it's important to honor and pay tribute to your beloved pet in a way that's right for you, it becomes even more crucial that you work with the right pet loss organization that will guide you and allow you to enjoy the rituals that you want.

Just like any service, there are some services that will be more suited to your needs. Unfortunately, there are some businesses that might not operate to the high level of standards that will be important to you at this emotional time. To be violated and used at such a difficult time can make a loss even tougher to deal with.

I'm embarrassed to admit it, but one of these examples is right in my backyard. Funeral home owner and director Rick Pyke, owner of R.D. Pyke Funeral Home, was arrested on charges of class D felony theft in May 2010 when undercover investigators conducted a sting operation. The investigators determined that Pyke, who offered a pet cremation service, took money from a grieving family mourning the loss of their dog. He gave them back some cremated remains even though he never did the cremation, according to published reports. A raid at Pyke's business discovered two badly decomposed animal carcasses.

Another example comes from Canada, where authorities shut down The Domestic Animal Cremation and Misty Gardens Pet Cemetery near La Salle, Manitoba. Investigators determined that the business was mishandling animal carcasses and operating under filthy conditions. Bodies were left rotting for months without being cremated.

These examples drastically hurt pet parents who specifically turned to professionals to have something more done for their pets. Many pet parents who have their pets euthanized at a veterinarian's office and expect the remains to be respectfully disposed of after death also suffer when they later find out that the remains were not treated with respect or dignity.

As pet parents, it is our duty, obligation, and responsibility to make sure that the services that veterinarians use are reputable and are handling our beloved pets in the way that we want them to be handled. As with our human loved ones, we would not just send their bodies off after death without understanding where they were going and how they were going to be treated.

One of my dear colleagues, Bill Remkus, owner of Hinsdale Animal Cemetery and Crematory in Willowbrook, Ill., and I constantly try to educate the public and the veterinary community about those firms that can be described as nothing other than "waste companies." These companies will incinerate animals en masse and simply dump the remains in landfills. In some cases, they won't cremate the bodies at all, dumping them on the side of the road or in illegal dumpsites.

Many times, pet parents who ask about how the remains of their pets are treated have been told something different than what actually occurs. In the truest form of education, it's important for everyone involved in the final arrangements of a pet's body to be educated on what the exact process is. Pet parents and many veterinarians agree that waste companies should not play a role in disposing our pets because the process should not even involve disposal; it should be a respectful form of disposition.

Remkus has been one of the most outspoken critics against waste companies and unethical operators in the pet cremation business. It was for this reason that I partnered with him to form the Pet Loss Professionals Alliance, which is a division of the International Cemetery, Cremation and Funeral Association. I'll speak more about the PLPA later, but suffice it to say that it's an association that seeks to create solid definitions, standards and an ethical code of practice. When pet parents work with a PLPA firm, they will know that they are more likely to be working with someone reputable.

However, even though the PLPA is growing, it will take us quite some time to make sure that pet care professionals, veterinarians and members of the public are educated, and I'm hoping that this book helps spread the word faster about the many reasons why it's important to give pet parents options in the loss of their pets. More pet crematories, veterinarians and pet memorial businesses and suppliers will join our network, and while you should not disqualify firms that have not yet joined, it's important to ask questions about their business practices. The important thing is that you make sure that the services you need, from respectful care of your pet to memorialization items to ritual services, can be provided by the company that you are considering. While the majority of pet loss professionals truly care about helping you in a time of need, you have the right to make sure that their business practices and range of services fit *your* needs.

I can't say it enough: The key is to educate yourself about the process to ensure that you are getting what you want and deserve.

Understanding Terminology

When you choose the pet crematory or pet funeral home that will be guiding you during the loss of your pet, I want to educate you on the definitions and terms that you will encounter during this process. I want you to be fully educated and versed in this area so that you can ask important questions to get the information and answers that are important to you. Here are some examples:

Private cremation: This involves the cremation of just one animal. The remains are placed in the retort and no other pets should be placed in the chamber until the crematory operator removes the remains of your pet.

A private cremation ensures that the cremated remains of your pet will not be commingled with the cremated remains of other pets.

Be sure, however, that when a business says that it is providing your pet with a "private cremation" that it is just that – private. You want to ensure that no other animals are in the cremation chamber at the time when your pet is also being cremated. Many firms will say that a cremation is "private" when really they are separating the remains of various animals with a barrier while cremating them at the same time. While it's important to know that many companies will use the word "private" in their cremation practices, it's more important for you to clarify that your pet will be ***the only one*** in the cremator at the time the cremation process is performed.

Segregated cremation (with ash return): With this type of cremation, two or more animals are placed in a cremator with bricks or some other barrier separating the remains. The crematory operator should monitor the cremation process. When collecting the remains, he or she will try to do everything possible to avoid commingling the cremated remains. However, there will be a high likelihood that the cremated remains will be commingled during the cremation process, and the cremated remains that you receive back may also have the ashes of the other animals that are in the retort at that time.

Communal or "Group" cremation: Some families opt to not get the ashes of their pet returned to them. In this instance, your pet's remains will be put into a cremation chamber with many other pets, but there will be nothing done to ensure that the remains are kept separate. With this process, there will not be an opportunity to get cremated remains back. Families wanting this process will want to know from their crematory provider or their veterinarian where the cremated remains will be spread or buried. Many pet crematories will dispose of these remains in a group cemetery plot honoring animals or will scatter these remains.

If your veterinarian is working with a reputable cremation provider, the above cremation processes will be how your pet will be handled. As a pet parent, you might also want to ask how your pet's body will be handled after death and before they get to the crematory. For many pet parents, they will want to know that the body is being cared for respectfully and not merely placed into a plastic bag, stacked with other animals in a freezer, and then thrown on a truck. If you want something different for your pet, much like I did and how I train other pet loss professionals to treat deceased pet bodies, make this known to the pet funeral home that you will be working with.

At the minimum, even with a communal cremation, you know that your animal's remains are being handled respectfully by a trained professional. You may encounter variations of these terms when working with a pet crematory or pet loss professional, but you should generally be able to narrow down the term so that it fits into one of the above definitions.

How to Educate Yourself on the Final Arrangement Process

With all aspects of the final arrangements of your pet, even if you do not plan to get the cremated remains of your pet back, you should ask how the remains of your pet will be handled. Here are some specific questions you might consider asking, either of your veterinarian or of the pet loss company that you will be working directly with:

- What pet cremation service do you work with?
- Are the cremations performed onsite of the pet loss company?
- Do you have a brochure or flier highlighting the business?
- If some kind of promotional material is not available, can I get the website address or phone number?
- What does their Pet Release and Cremation Authorization form look like?
- If you want to witness the cremation process, can you?
- If you want to take a tour of the facility where the remains of your pet are being handled, can you? Does the facility have an open door policy so that you might visit their facility at any time?
- What are the various cremation processes that they do?
- What is the identification process that the crematory uses to ensure it is your pet's cremated remains that you get back?
- How long will it be before your pet's body is picked up – if the facility is picking your pet up at the veterinary clinic?

- Can you get the cremated remains of your pet back? If so, how long will it take to get the remains back?
- If you opt to get cremated remains back, will they be the remains of your pet? How are you assured of that?
- If you don't opt to get the cremated remains back, how will the remains ultimately be disposed?
- What other services are offered? Does the business offer grief support?
- What memorialization items are available?

I know so many pet parents who may not have wanted to receive the remains back but neither did they want the remains of their beloved pet to end up in a landfill or some other place that did not honor their pet or pets in general. Ask questions!

Pet Memorialization Items

For many pet parents, the death of a pet will be the first time that they have experienced a loss, and therefore, they might not know what their options are for memorialization products. I find the various memorialization products interesting and meaningful in celebrating and honoring the life that I have shared with my pets.

Let me educate you on some of the things that you can do to honor your precious pet. While this is certainly not an exhaustive list of everything that's available, I'd like to guide you on some of the pieces that have been special to me, some of the items that I've helped families with in creating memorials for their pets, and, in general, ideas for you, your family and your friends in remembering a special pet.

For my journey, I wanted to honor Mico in a variety of ways, including through jewelry. Around my neck I wear a charm that has her paw print on it, a beautiful silver charm on a silver necklace. My wonderful friend and colleague, David Gordon of Buddies, actually takes the paw print of a pet, shrinks it down and then engraves it onto a charm. This company is phenomenal as it has created some of the most unusual, special and creative memorialization jewelry pieces.

For Mike the Dog, my husband loved his big Golden Retriever pink nose! Therefore, it was only fitting for him to get cuff links with Mike's nose print on them. Are you aware that animal nose prints are like our thumb prints, no two are alike? The nose print is the animal's individuality! The cuff links are priceless.

This company will also take human fingerprints, hand prints, baby's feet, bird claws, and horse's hooves and create rings, earrings, lighters, key chains, family pendants, and many other personalized jewelry pieces. You've already learned about Dr. Shelly Zacharias and her love for her pets. With every pet that dies for Shelly, she adds this pet's paw print charm to a "mommy's bracelet" that she started when Macy and Caddy Jo died. The bracelet is gorgeous – and so special for Shelly.

Also, for me, I like to know that I have the spirit of all of my pets with me when I travel, teach and consult. Therefore, when I need the strength of all of my pets, I'll wear a necklace that has the fur of all of my pets, living and deceased. Oh, the wonderful confidence that it gives to me to know that I have them all with me and am delivering my training, teaching and work on their behalf.

There are so many beautiful designs for cremation jewelry on the market now. Many cremation jewelry pieces truly look like works of art versus vessels to hold cremated remains. However, these pieces don't have to be meant solely for a deceased pet's cremated remains or hair. They can also be wonderful vessels to hold a living pet's hair.

When it comes to deciding on an urn for a pet, much like I've guided you in the Planning Ahead section, there are so many options available. The urns will vary in material from:

- Marble
- Ceramic
- Metal
- Wood
- Copper
- Bronze
- Rocks

Deciding on an urn is going to be very much of a personal preference. This will depend on depicting the personality of your pet to making sure the urn fits within your home's décor.

In deciding on an urn, you might also want to think about personalizing the piece. On many of these pieces, you have the option of engraving. The engraving might be the pet's name, their nicknames, or a sentiment much like an epitaph that you want to remember your pet by.

Another wonderful idea is to get rocks or markers to honor your pets in the outdoors. My dogs love to be outside. Therefore, I have strategically placed rocks around my flower beds and in those special areas where they like to lay in soaking up the sunshine or by a tree that provided hours of entertainment as a place to chase squirrels.

I remember one family I assisted with their beautiful chow, Bubba. As a family, this was their second dog to die. Their first dog died in the winter, therefore, they planted a winter-tolerant bush and placed next to it a special rock in honor of that pet. Bubba died in the fall. They planted a beautiful mum plant, with a rock next to it that acknowledged the season of his death.

For some families, their animals liked to be in the outside elements. If this is the case, then look for an urn that can go outside. Another dear colleague of mine, David Link with Ceramica and Keepstones, actually worked with me in creating a rock urn for those that wanted to bury the ashes but also wanted to know that if they moved, the ashes could then be moved with the family. David has actually crafted an actual river rock into an urn by preparing the back of the rock to hold a weather and element resistant "urn," and then engraving the front of the rock with a special meaning. It is a perfect option for people who want more of a natural element for an urn that reflects the raw nature that our pets represent.

Art pieces are another way to honor a pet, from painted art pieces to any other type of medium that works within your home's décor. There are also options to have sculptures made in the likeness of your pet. Many of these sculptures can also be used as urns.

While many pet parents have pets that are "mutts" – it's important for us that we have opportunities to personalize a piece with our pet's own photo. There are so many products that can incorporate your pet's photo to make it truly special. There are:

- Blankets
- Purses
- Pillows
- Jewelry
- Charms
- Bronze markers
- Artwork
- Note cards

For many of the items that I have mentioned to you, you don't have to wait until the pet has died to have these pieces. They are all more than acceptable to get before your pet has died. I love honoring all of my pets – *every day!*

Final Thoughts

With the situation outlined above, as well as various other situations in pet loss practices, it is for this reason that I, once again, strongly encourage you to ask questions. If you are turning to your veterinarian to guide you, find out what company he or she works with after your pet dies. If you aren't happy with what you hear, explore other options. It's incredibly important for you to find the pet loss team and organization that will treat not only your pet but you with the dignity and respect that is deserved at a time like this.

Also, be sure that you let your veterinarian know that it is important to you that they work with a firm that operates ethically and one that will respect the remains of your pet. Veterinarians focus on keeping your pet alive, and that is their specialty, so they are not accustomed to thinking how they can best serve their customers after an animal dies. Many veterinarians – even very good ones – will opt to work with the cheapest pet cremation or disposal service because they have no clue how much their clients value knowing that their pets are treated well in death, just as they were treated in life.

Memorialization Options To Honor Your Pet

Standard Charm

CHAPTER 6

How a Stray Dog Became "Daddy's Boy"

Squirty smiles for the camera.

I turned in early that night knowing I'd need all my energy the next day for the Humane Society's Annual Celebration of Life Memorial Service. It was going to be an emotional day laced with the most beautiful stories, with pet parents supporting each other and paying tribute to those precious pets who had died. As the director of the service, I wanted to be prepared.

The service needed to help people tell their stories and deal with their emotions. Fresh, I needed to be fresh.

But at 2:30 a.m., the first call of the night came in. I had been sound asleep for a few hours, so it took me a minute to gather myself, reach for the phone, and get myself prepared. When someone calls me at this time of night, it usually isn't good.

As usual, I cleared my throat and groggily picked up the phone. "This is Coleen," I managed to squeak out.

The person on the other end of the line paused for a long moment, but when he finally began speaking, I could immediately tell from his voice that this call was going to be like so many others I had received so early in the morning.

"Um . . . This is Steve Cardwell. I am at the emergency clinic with my boy, Squirty. He just . . . ."

The tears started to come. To say that word for the first time is more than a pet parent can do. The reality of that word. The realization that saying the word, "died" makes it all true. That realization, that fact of life, is more than any pet parent can ever handle without support.

I assured Steve that I was there for him and that we would take as long as needed to get through the call. "It's OK," I said. "Catch your breath; I'm here when you're ready. Just take your time."

There was a moment when he still didn't talk. "Steve, I'm so sorry," I said.

Those words, too, were more than what Steve was ready to hear. He did not want anyone to be sorry for him. He just wanted his Squirty back. He wanted to go back to "normal," but that was before he made this phone call. I knew that I was the last person in the world that he wanted to talk to.

I sat on my bed listening to the silence on the line for what seemed like hours even though it was only a minute or two. Finally, it was clear to Steve that he couldn't choke out any more words. I finally heard him say, "Here's my wife."

The phone was fumbled around and then a woman's clear voice came on. It was evident that she had assumed the role of being in charge. "Hi. This is Shawn, Steve's wife," she said.

"Hi, Honey. Tell me what's going on."

"We're at the emergency clinic on Bash Street right now," she said. "Our little guy, Squirty, has been struggling for a bit, and tonight we had to bring him in."

I listened intently to gather in as much information as I could because I knew the conversation was probably going to be short. I knew that both Steve and his wife were going to try avoiding certain words and would have a hard time expressing what they were feeling. The phrase "bring him in," for instance, was just a way to avoid saying that as they were driving, they knew it would be their last ride with Squirty. It was going to take some time to come to terms with what happened, and no one is ever prepared to go through it. The reality that an unconditional love is truly gone is more than the heart can process. The reality that a chapter of your life is over and that the rest of the story will forever be changed can be seemingly impossible to comprehend.

While I had no clue at that point the specific circumstances of this family's life with their loved pet, I kept hearing one statement loud and clear: "He is our baby."

I knew that this little guy had truly brought love and happiness to Steve and Shawn. I knew that there would be a story about this little boy and, and I was so anxious to hear and honor that story.

Shawn continued with some of the technical details. "He's here at the clinic on his bed and in a sea of blankets. He just loves blankets and is snuggled among them, just as he loves to do. We will keep those here with him. Please make sure that you keep those blankets with him when you get him."

I assured her that the clinic was very respectful of the pets' bodies. I knew that the staff there would keep the blankets with Squirty until my arrival later on in the morning. For me, the dignity and the respect of a deceased body are of the utmost importance. That was my mission, and I was going to make sure to make it happen.

I confirmed that Steve and Shawn had completed the necessary paperwork with the clinic that would allow staff members to release the body to me. I assured both of them that I would be there the next morning and would call them when I safely had Squirty with me.

As Shawn was about to hang up the phone, I heard Steve in the background asking to speak to me again. He got on the phone, tears in his voice, and quietly asked me to take care of "his boy." I assured him that I would treat him just like my own.

I also told him that I would be checking in with them in the morning when Squirty was with me. With that phone call, we would then make our way through more of the final arrangements. So early in the morning and after being hit with such a devastating loss, there was nothing more that they needed to do but go home. I knew they would not get any sleep as they faced their first night without their little guy. But I was hoping they would at least be able to get some rest and be able to comfort each other in the privacy of their own home.

I asked to speak to the clinic team again to confirm with them that I would be there in the morning. After hanging up the phone, I placed my head back on the pillow, trying to fall back asleep. As tired as I was, my heart broke for Steve and Shawn and for a love that was now gone. It is a hurt that I know all too well.

As I did for any family that I companion through a journey of grief, I said a quick prayer for them before I drifted off. I wanted them to find peace.

Picking Up Squirty

Morning came quickly, and Chris and I headed to the emergency clinic to get Squirty. As we made our way there, my mind went over the call from earlier in the morning, and my heart broke in two again.

We got to the clinic and found Squirty just like Shawn said. That scruffy little guy was lying in the most adorable little bed and was snuggled in a sea of blankets. I looked at his face and saw peace, love and content. I imagined him, full of life, burrowing in these blankets, looking out at Steve and Shawn with a smile on his face and a look that said, "I am so happy!" Looking at the face of a deceased pet always makes my heart swell with love as I realize that I have just been entrusted with a family's precious cargo. In these faces, I see a life full of stories and unconditional love.

Chris scooped Squirty up in his arms, and we made our way to the truck. We got Squirty safely placed in, careful not to disturb him in his bed and blankets. We made our way to the memorial center. But even before we set out on the road, I placed a call to the Cardwells. Steve answered the phone.

"Steve, it's Coleen."

"Hi," he said. "How are you?"

"Well, it's not about me right now. It's all about you and Shawn. How are you guys?"

That is generally all it takes for a flood of emotion and words to begin tumbling out. I listened until there was a break in the conversation and a time that I knew Steve was ready for me to take over and to begin taking care of them. I knew they would want no part in carrying out Squirty's final arrangements, but they would want input in determining how to pay tribute to their beloved pet. They needed someone to begin guiding them during these final arrangements and a myriad of options and decisions, all of which they wanted no part of. And they would need certain information to get through the next few days.

"First of all, I wanted you to know that Squirty is with me, safe and sound right now," I said. "He's in his bed and blankets, just like you left him last night. And, he's very much at peace. What a beautiful boy he is!"

There were sniffles at the other end of the line as the reality of this situation continued to sink in. As with most pet parents, Steve and Shawn let me know that they didn't really know what their choices were now that Squirty had died, and they had no clue where to go from here.

As a person who can really understand people and their emotions, I felt that it would help Steve and Shawn to come see Squirty again. To have this special being just ripped away from them without spending some time with him again just did not seem like the best course of action. As with the loss of any love in our life, it is important to at least have the opportunity to spend some time with a deceased loved one. Not for closure but to take the time to back up, say hello again, and begin to get prepared for the final goodbye. The Cardwells definitely needed that time with Squirty. However, just like most pet parents, they did not even know it.

"Steve, during this time that we will be spending together in making the final arrangements for Squirty, I am going to guide you and to do some of your thinking for you," I said. "At a time like this, you feel naked and vulnerable in not knowing what to do and what your options are. In addition, we are not going to move forward in what we need to do until I feel like you are ready for the next steps. At this moment, there is not one decision that needs to be made by you and Shawn, so you can relax." I then added, "What I feel you should both do right now is see Squirty again and spend some time with him. From there, we will take baby steps and decide what we need to do."

"Really, I can see him again?" Steve asked. "I didn't know that was possible." After thinking for a moment, he added, "I don't even know if that's what I want to do."

"Steve, I can tell you that of all of the people that I have made this recommendation to, not one of them has ever come back to me and said, 'I wish I wouldn't have done that,'" I told him. "In fact, it has been the contrary. When your heart is ready, you will look back on this time together again and you will be so thankful that you had some time together, outside of the clinic, and to see Squirty in a peaceful setting."

Steve thought about this for a brief moment. "Can we come up this afternoon to see him?"

"Absolutely," I told him. And knowing that I had to direct the Humane Society's Celebration of Life Memorial Service, I timed the visitation accordingly. "We'll see you at the center at 3:00 this afternoon, Steve."

Celebrating Pets with the Humane Society

The Humane Society's Celebration Paws & Remember was a beautiful service. It was truly a safe place for people to come and to be with others whose hearts were also breaking due to the loss of a special pet. There were families, single parents, sons and mothers, daughters and fathers, and couples – all coming together for one reason. As they came into the service, a beautiful video was playing that my stepson, Brian, had put together for the event. The video included photos that each attendee had sent in of their special pet. The photos scrolling on the screen set to some incredibly touching music made for an amazing masterpiece! There were cats, dogs, bunnies, and birds – all magnificently stunning! It was so touching to watch each of the attendees paying attention, just waiting for their beloved pet's photo to roll across the screen. When it did, they touched their neighbor, pointed to the screen, smiled, cried, and acted as if their child had just appeared in a Grammy winning movie. And, it was true – these beautiful little creatures *were* stars in a movie that would forever play on in their hearts.

Walking a bit further into the room, each family made their way to the far side of the service to a table. At this table, they were given the opportunity to light a candle and write a note. Pet parents placed toys, urns and flowers as well as sealed envelopes containing special private messages. When all of the candles were lit and the table was full of special mementos, the site became truly ethereal and spiritual. One could just feel the air changing with the love flowing out of each and every person that was there.

Readings were read, names of the deceased pets were said aloud, and tears were shed. As I looked out into the audience, people held photos of their special friends to their hearts, and it was clear that their broken hearts would never be the same again. It was such a glorious occasion – one that was laden with tears but also one that told each person there, "please mourn and pay honor to this love that you have lost." I was so proud of my Humane Society for giving these people the permission to share those emotions and feelings.

The service became even more touching when one of our local TV anchors read a moving poem in memory of her little Oliver, then went through the shelter and opened her heart again to adopting a new love.

Building Up the Courage to Say Goodbye

When the service wrapped up, Chris and I headed to the center to meet Steve and Shawn. As we pulled the truck to the back of the center, I noticed a couple sitting on a bench in front of the complex. I immediately knew from the look on their faces that these were the grieving pet parents.

We put Squirty in the chapel and made sure that his blankets and bed were appropriately fluffed, and as soon as we had finished, the front bell rang. I left Chris to do the final touches, and I made my way to the gallery area of the center. Ah, yes, I recognized "the look." I grabbed Steve and gave him a hug, which then turned into more of a hold. Steve held on tightly, letting the tears flow.

"I'm so sorry," I said. It was such a small statement but no other words were appropriate. I then turned to Shawn and gave her a hug, too. They were both grieving but it was already clear that Squirty was certainly a "Daddy's boy." I knew the journey of grief with Steve would be a rocky one.

It was time to lead Steve and Shawn in to see Squirty. I explained to them a bit about a deceased body and what they would be seeing. They were ready and anxious to see their boy, and when we stepped into the chapel, I audibly heard their gasps. "Oh my gosh – there's our boy."

Together we walked to his body. I was the first to pat him on the head, and then I quietly slipped away to make room for Steve and Shawn to be near their precious love. They both leaned down and began talking to Squirty, and they showered his head with little kisses. Oh my; this was a loved little scruffy dog!

Steve and Shawn spent a lot of time with Squirty that afternoon. Telling stories and reliving memories. Sharing with Chris and me how this feisty dog showed up at their doorstep many houses ago as a stray. He made himself at home and quickly crawled into their hearts.

There were tears. There were smiles. And there was a bit of laughter. Exhausted and emotionally drained, Steve and Shawn eventually decided that they were ready to leave. But when I asked them if they were ready to move forward with the cremation, I saw them hesitate.

"Steve, as I had mentioned, I am going to offer you some options – options that I would want if I were in your shoes," I said. "I had told you that there was nothing that we needed to do right now. Why don't you come back and see Squirty again before we go to cremation? I just feel like you need a bit more time with him."

Steve and Shawn wholeheartedly agreed. Being in tune with her husband's best interests, Shawn felt like Steve needed some solo time with Squirty, so we arranged for that to happen. Steve did need to be out of town on business during the week, but we were able to make it work. We prepared Squirty's body for holding and had him ready for Steve to see at the end of the week.

I spent a lot of time on the phone with Steve that week, helping him through his journey. The feelings and emotional rollercoaster are always wild during these first few days, and Steve's journey was no different. My heart ached for him, as I knew he was on the road on business and struggling to concentrate. At the end of the week, he would come back home and have to enter a home without his Squirty. At least he would be able to spend some more time with him, albeit in a state that he would rather not have. It was all bittersweet.

That last visit with Steve and Squirty was incredibly moving. I had put them in the family room so that they could have their privacy and so a conversation could be held just between a daddy and his boy. When Steve came out of the room, I could tell that it had been tough. There would never be enough time for all of the words, but then again, there was not enough emotional capacity for any more words.

Clearly Steve and Shawn's life will be forever changed because of this stray dog that showed up on their doorstep years ago. This little dog taught them how to be feisty, how to survive, how to forgive and how to love. This little dog ended up stealing both of their hearts.

While Steve was still heartbroken, he knew it was time to move forward. He had been given a beautiful opportunity of saying "hello" to Squirty, and now he was ready to begin his grief journey in saying goodbye.

In closing, it's always so heartwarming to hear from a family after I've had the privilege of helping them with a beloved pet. The following letter still reduces me to tears every time I read it. It is a constant reminder of why I chose to be a pet loss professional. Thanks, Steve, for sharing your heart with me – and more importantly, your beautiful boy, Squirty.

A Letter from Steve Cardwell to Coleen Ellis

Coleen,

I have been writing this letter for days now. I have been unable to get very far with this letter because I am still grieving for my little boy, Squirty. But I need to tell you how much I appreciate you and your business. My wife is writing a similar note, using her own words, so don't be confused if I switch between the pronouns "I" and "we."

I have told dozens of people about you and your business and I usually start off with saying, "There is a special place in heaven for Coleen . . ." What I mean by that statement is the warmth in your heart, your sincere desire to help, your capacity for understanding the pain people are going through, and the fact that you have chosen a business of helping people and pets deal with the afterlife. That choice of business cannot be easy and I am sure you have tough days. Tough days like seeing a 250 pound, giant, bald man break down and cry over a scruffy little dog.

You have helped us (more than you will ever know) through these dark days. For example, you had never met me; I was taken aback when you instantly gave me a hug. You whispered to me that you were sorry about Squirty as if we had been friends for years. That quality in a person is rare, and I wanted to let you know how much I appreciate you.

Right now my emotions are rather scrambled with Squirty's long illness and eventual death. However, there are two distinct parts of my personality that are surfacing throughout this whole process. First, the grieving parent. Squirty was a little "person" that showed me the value and the innocence of unconditional love. Squirty taught me a lot of things, but most of all he taught me how to take the time to enjoy the simple things in life. For example, a spot of sunshine, a fresh scent in the air, mud puddles, warm blankets, and lounging around the house on rainy days! Most of all, Squirty taught me the value of showing someone how much you appreciate their kindness.

The other part of my brain is thinking about your business. How owning and running the business must be tough. Also, how the type of business is needed and how it is imperative that your business prospers. I was trying to think how I could show my gratitude for your business, and after dozens of bad ideas, the only good idea finally came to me. I would like to offer any of your potential customers to contact me. I mean day or night, work or on vacation, anytime or anywhere. I would gladly speak with them about my experience with you and your business. I will tell them that if I had to do it all over again, I would have contacted you sooner! The sincere sharing of your experience, those of your other customers, and the advice you have given us have <u>helped us immensely.</u> Every suggestion you have made was wise and thoughtful. Your suggestions were offered to me humbly and always with the caveat that you will do whatever I truly want with Squirt's arrangements and that you are there to help me.

The two parts of my personality, the "parent" and the "business person" were both very impressed with you and your business.

I have never before written a thank you note to the owner of a business. And since you are more to us than just a business owner, I guess that trend continues. However, I would just like to say, from the bottom of my grieving heart, thank you for all your kindness and help.

Sincerely,
Steven N. Cardwell.

P.S.: Specific things we are thankful for:

- *You being so sweet when you received the 2:30 a.m. phone call when Squirt passed. I honestly thought I was calling your answering service!*
- *Letting us see him on a Sunday, and when you were so busy. We never even thought to ask if you were going to be open that day.*
- *The time needed to spend with him before cremation. You had suggested it; I never thought I would want it, now it is the single most important part in my grieving. Thank you again!*
- *All the stories you shared with us. You are so busy (because you are helping so many people) so we really appreciate the time.*

Coleen Shares Lessons Learned with Shawn, Steve and Other Pet Parents

Dear Shawn and Steve:

As I look back on our time together in honoring Squirty, I wanted to share with others what I learned from you that would help other pet parents in deciding what they want to do to honor their beloved pet. You did such a great job in pinpointing what you learned from the process, that I thought other pet parents would appreciate your insights.

You said time and time again how you wished you would've made the phone call sooner to learn of your options. Consider preplanning efforts for your pet. Begin thinking about what you would like to do for their final arrangements.

If you "don't know what you don't know" as far as your options, think about your own human loss situations and what rituals are important to you and your family in these processes.

Educate yourself on the various options that are available. Really look at these options and ask yourself, "What is right for our family and how we pay tribute to our pet?"

Reach out to the firms in your area to determine what their services are and how they match up with what your wishes are.

Call these firms and ask them questions. Ask them a lot of questions.

Don't ask these firms for permission to honor your pet, for permission to pay tribute to your pet, in whatever way you want to pay tribute. TELL them this is what you want to do.

And, lastly, when you are looking for a place that you will entrust your special pet's final arrangements too, find a pet loss professional whose personality and mission in caring for deceased loved ones matches with yours as well.

Thank you for letting me share Squirty's story. I am humbled to honor him and the love that you both had for him.

Continued Peace to You,
Coleen

CHAPTER 7

Finding the Right Cemetery for Your Pet

A statue at Hinsdale Animal Cemetery and Crematory in Illinois honors all pets buried there.

Not everyone wishes to cremate their pet, and pet cemeteries have been around for hundreds of years. This is another important area to learn about when considering the memorial options for your pet.

There are hundreds of pet cemeteries throughout the United States that continue the tradition of serving pet parents. Honoring and memorializing pets is not a new thing. The ancient Egyptians, for example, revered cats as sacred beings and often took great care in memorializing the pets belonging to a pharaoh or other member of a royal family or placing statues of their likeness in the pyramids.

While many of the families I work with choose to cremate their pets and keep those remains in an urn that they keep close to them, there are still many families that want to bury their pet in a pet cemetery or inter the cremated remains in a mausoleum at a pet cemetery. Many human cemeteries now have pet sections, and in some states, a pet parent can even choose to have the remains of their pet buried with their own remains upon their death in the same cemetery space. One of my colleagues, Tom Flynn with Hillcrest-Flynn Memorial Park in Hermitage, Pa., tells me the People and Pet Gardens section at his cemetery is a popular option among pet parents. In this section of his cemetery, people can be buried right next to their pet. This is a new type of cemetery in the United States and one that I'm sure will grow in popularity as pet parents more fully explore and request different options in death care.

Other human cemeteries are creating pet sections to help serve their customers, but there are also a wide and diverse array of cemeteries that cater specifically to pets and pets alone. As with any type of death-care operation, the consumer needs to make sure that he or she is working with a reputable firm.

There are entire associations devoted to pet cemeteries. Most, if not all, of the cemeteries that belong to the International Association of Pet Cemeteries have been in operation for a long time and are reputable. The Pet Loss Professionals Alliance, a division of the International Cemetery, Cremation and Funeral Association, also can put consumers in contact with a reputable cemetery that serves pets. I am the PLPA's director, and it has been my pleasure to help various pet cemeteries and other pet loss operations refine their businesses to improve the services that they provide to families.

Choose Carefully

Throughout my years in this business, I've seen too many families heartbroken after being told they could no longer visit the grave of a pet because the cemetery changes owners. Unlike human cemeteries, pet cemeteries are often not as protected, and there are not as many rules.

I've already touched upon the fact that some pet cemeteries are not properly operated, and you have to ask the right questions to ensure you are working with a good operation. I share with you the following stories, not to alarm you but to make you aware of some situations that have happened across the United States to pet parents:

- Almost 200 pet caskets had to be removed from Thistlerose Pet Cemetery in Greendale, Wis., in 2009. When the owner of the cemetery died, the 1.8-acre property was sold.

The cemetery owner's family wanted to keep the cemetery operating, but a number of factors prevented that from happening. They did pay for the remains of the pets to be removed and returned for those pet parents who chose to move their pets. But it was a circumstance that many pet parents never foresaw, and it reopened a lot of wounds.

- In Florence, Ala., dozens of people buried their pets in a cemetery off of Hough Road behind a Walmart. But the land was turned over to a mortgage company after the owner died. Owners had to spend a day exhuming the remains of their pets on their own. Heavy equipment operators cleared the land upon the change in ownership, and some pet owners found out about what was going on too late to remove the remains of their beloved pets.

- Paradise Pet Ranch in Palm Beach, Fla., was destroyed and replaced with condominiums in 2007 after years of neglect. The property wasn't deeded to forever be a pet cemetery, and so developers had the right to build. At least the condominium operator planned to post a notice in the newspaper to allow pet owners to retrieve remains before the condominiums were built.

Owners of pet cemeteries who get in financial trouble and who sell or lose land can put a pet cemetery in a tough spot, and it's the bereaved pet owners who end up suffering. If you aren't working with the right business, you also risk having your pet buried in a mismarked grave or the remains could be poorly handled.

But don't be discouraged! While there are fewer regulations governing pet funeral homes, cremation services and pet cemeteries than there are for human businesses, there are so many great businesspeople out there who are pet lovers themselves and who are want to serve their clients the right way. It's just a matter of seeking them out and knowing what questions to ask.

One of the best pet cemeteries in the United States is Hinsdale Animal Cemetery in Willowbrook, Ill., which is operated by my friend Bill Remkus. I've had the pleasure of knowing Bill for a number of years, and he serves as co-chairperson of the Pet Loss Professionals Alliance.

Hinsdale Animal Cemetery, established in 1926, is the final resting place for thousands of beloved pets. The grounds are beautifully maintained, and the Remkus family has always appreciated the special bond that exists between humans and their companion animals.

Hinsdale Animal Cemetery offers the following services, and these may give you some ideas on what to look for when it comes to finding a pet cemetery that meets your standards:

Private Burial: Single or multiple plots are available; families can select from a variety of wooden boxes and pet caskets.

Preplanning: Families are also given the option of preplanning for their pets. It's incredibly touching for me to walk through Bill's cemetery and see the various monuments and moving epitaphs. One pet mommy that I met at the cemetery was tending the six graves of her deceased pets. I walked with her as she told me the names and a bit about all of the pets that were interred at the cemetery. The last monument, for Maggie, was missing a death date. She had prepurchased this plot and the matching monument so that when that time came, Maggie would reside in death with her brothers and sisters.

Maintaining an immaculately manicured cemetery is important for the Remkus family. Renting shepherd hooks and providing seasonal flowers for sale to families ensures that the cemetery is always in a state of beauty.

Interestingly enough, the cremated remains of about 35 people rest at the Hinsdale Animal Cemetery as well. These pet lovers decided during the preplanning process that they wanted to be inurned with their pets at a pet cemetery instead of at a human cemetery. They made a great choice, because this pet cemetery and others like it are beautiful.

The cemetery also offers a variety of memorialization options, such as cremation jewelry, garden memorials for home, a variety of caskets, urns and other options. Some families choose beautiful granite monuments and headstones to memorialize a beloved pet.

There are hundreds of reputable pet cemeteries throughout the country – not just Hinsdale. For many families, having a place where they can go to remember their pet is important. Pet cemeteries can be a great option for families.

Here are some tips from Jonathan Remkus with Hinsdale Animal Cemetery on what types of questions families should ask when working with a pet cemetery:

1. Does the pet cemetery have a dedicated perpetual care fund?

A perpetual care fund pays for a minimal level of maintenance as well as taxes should the business fail, Jon said. "This money should remain separate from any general fund and be earmarked for no other use," he said. "This cannot be stressed enough."

It is shocking, but many pet cemeteries do not have an organized maintenance program, Jon said. "If clients do not select a perpetual care option or if it is not required, it is important for the cemetery to collect an annual maintenance fee for each grave," he said. If you are required to pay such a fee, it should not be excessive.

"Families should ask about perpetual care options and what should happen in the event that the business fails," Jon said. "It's not scientific, but families should go with their gut. If something doesn't seem right or answers aren't forthcoming, they might want to explore other options."

In the future, Jon hopes that states set minimum levels of perpetual care funding per acre or burial for pet cemeteries. "But like many other laws already on the books, they would be useless without enforcement," he said. "Few bureaucracies are going to want the added responsibilities, particularly without additional funding. I also would have concerns about how seriously a government agency would take their duties."

2. Is the pet cemetery in question a member of the Pet Loss Professionals Alliance?

Ask the business about its professional affiliations. Don't be afraid to check with the Pet Loss Professionals Alliance or even your local Better Business Bureau to verify that the pet cemetery you are working with is a member in good standing.

The PLPA can be contacted at 800-645-7700.

3. Can you tour the facilities?

Jon said that this is a must if you truly care about where your pet will be buried. "If the place looks inadequately maintained or run-down, or if it is difficult to get in contact with the company, you should use caution before burying a pet here," he said.

Some pet parents may decide they'd rather just bury a pet at their home, but this might become problematic if you ever move and want to continue visiting a pet's grave. If you have a marker of some sort, it might even make it harder to sell your home. Working with a reputable pet cemetery is a great option, and there are some great operations out there ready to serve your needs.

If you choose to go the home burial route, Jon said you should check with a municipal or county government office or consult your state Environmental Protection Agency or Department of Agriculture for guidance. "In most cases, burial of a pet at home is permissible, but owners should look toward the future and think about what might happen to the pet if they move or redevelop the property," he said.

When it comes to working with a pet cemetery, families in the end must demonstrate some level of trust. Aside from looking at the pet cemetery's balance sheets, the only other way for it to demonstrate a permanent commitment to being a cemetery is by having land-deed restrictions placed upon the property, Jon said. "You are going to have to trust that the ownership has indeed done this," he said.

In conclusion, by being educated on cemetery protocol, asking the right questions and touring the pet cemetery, you will be taking important steps to determine how best to proceed in memorializing and honoring your pet.

CHAPTER 8

Celebrating Moet

Debbie Lucas celebrates Christmas with her dog, Moet.

The door to the center opened and an incredibly distraught woman walked in. It was clear that something terrible had happened, and she was in a complete state of shock. It was day after Thanksgiving and even though it was a bit cloudy outside, she was wearing sunglasses. It was clear she was trying to hide from reality.

I immediately went up to her and gave her a hug. Her body language was one of shock, denial, and deep anger. She was not receptive to my hug because, clearly, she did not even want to be in the building. However, she had to find someone, anyone to help her with the unthinkable.

I guided her to the table and motioned for her to be seated. Knowing that she had to make the first move, I put my hand on hers and sat there for what seemed like hours. When I sensed that she was ready to talk and open up, I calmly said, "Tell me what's going on."

"My name is Debbie Lucas and my little girl is over at the emergency clinic," she said. "She couldn't fight anymore, and I took her in yesterday."

I began to piece the puzzle together myself. I had received a phone call that morning from Kathleen, a pet sitter in the area as well as a beautiful woman who volunteered at our pet funeral home to conduct our pet loss support groups. Debbie had called her earlier in the morning because she needed someone to help her deal with the loss of her dog, Moet, a beautiful little Bichon Frise who she had named after her favorite champagne. Debbie had called her normal veterinary clinic in the morning asking for some help, and the staff there had told her about Kathleen and our pet loss support groups.

Kathleen knew that Debbie needed more for Moet if she were to truly deal with her loss. Debbie had treasured Moet as if she were her child ever since she got her as a puppy. The two had gone through so much together, and Debbie had tried everything to save Moet from the bladder cancer that became too much for her dog to bear. Moet passed away on Thanksgiving night in 2004.

Moet was Debbie's entire world. She needed the opportunity to do more for Moet, to do everything she could to honor the great bond that they shared. In closing our conversation, Kathleen said, "I know that she needs you right now, Coleen. If anyone needs to do a memorial service for their precious fur baby, it's Debbie. Be expecting a call."

Well, here was "the call." In front of me was such a visible sign of pain that it hurt my heart. Moet had been through so many of life's experiences with Debbie – a divorce, different jobs, and every other surprise life had to offer. After a few minutes of talking to her, I discovered just how much this woman who had never had children loved Moet.

Soon, Debbie pulled out a photo album from her purse, stuffed to the point of overflowing with photos of this little creature. One photo showed Moet in a nurse's hat for Debbie's graduation as a registered nurse. In every single photo where the two were pictured together, there was a big smile on Debbie's face. I realized that every moment that Debbie spent with Moet really was a celebration, and the dog couldn't have been named any better.

A great weight was taken off of Debbie's shoulders once she learned she could pay tribute to Moet and honor her remains respectfully. "I had gone home the night Moet died, and I thought it was just horrible that this little love of my life just gets picked up in a truck and goes to somewhere that I don't know about, and that I could only hope to get her ashes back," she told me. It quickly became clear that Debbie did not want her beloved little pet at that clinic, in a garbage bag, in a freezer, being treated so differently than she enjoyed being treated by Debbie. That one point was clear. From there, she had no idea what to do.

I told Debbie that I was going to make sure that Moet was picked up from that clinic respectfully. I left her to her thoughts at the table, jumped up and quickly got my stepson Brian on the road to the emergency clinic. There, he wrapped her snuggly in a blanket and put her beautiful little body in a casket with the dignity and respect that she deserved.

When I returned to the table, Debbie quietly asked, "Why didn't my veterinarian tell me about you? Why didn't they tell me about you last night at the emergency clinic? Why?"

I told Debbie that it wasn't the time to focus on others but that she needed to focus on herself and what was best for Moet. But I knew that she was upset, and that if the topic came up again, she was still not going to be pleased with how the situation was handled. She was angry that she was not given options when she, as a pet parent, was clearly one that would want and need these options.

I was ready to begin discussing with Debbie our next step to memorialize Moet and to pay honor to her life. "I think that it might be nice to have a memorial service for Moet," I said. "She obviously has touched many people in her life, as well as being such a large part of your life, that it would be nice to have everyone come together."

"Do people do that? Do they have funerals for their pets?" she asked.

"What is it that *you* want to do, Debbie?" I asked. "This is really all about what you want for Moet, and for you."

"Yes," she said emphatically. "That is what I want to do then. That is what she deserves. She deserves it all."

"Let's just start working through the service details then. This service will be all about Moet and honoring the special little life that she led. Let's pull together people, readings, and some special time together that will let everyone show their support and come together as a group that loved this little dog."

From there, we began to work through the details of the service. The process did not happen entirely that afternoon as Debbie was trying to work through her emotions at the same time she decided how to best honor Moet. As she planned the service, I discovered how much Moet meant to so many people. Debbie had to travel extensively for her job, and one of her good friends often took care of Moet when she was away. In fact, this friend was joined by her husband to visit Moet on Thanksgiving night when it was clear her time was up.

The Service

Debbie was like so many other pet parents. She felt that if she stopped for a minute and let her brain take over, she would collapse into a heap, possibly never to get up again and function in the world as she knew it today. It was work trying to find things to occupy and distract her. If reality took over, it would be unbearable.

The next few days were spent in not only helping other families but also being there for Debbie. There were phone calls and there were spontaneous visits to Pet Angel Memorial Center. Often, Debbie would just drop by with something and say, "I had to drop these toys by for Moet's service" or she'd share an idea about the service and want to know what I thought about it. These visits brought Debbie to a safe place to show her emotions. At the center, she could openly mourn, be angry or just check in on Moet, who was resting peacefully. Debbie knew that because I loved pets and because I was taking care of Moet's body, she could come to the center and show her emotions without being ashamed.

The service came together beautifully. The readings were going to be exactly what Debbie needed to hear for comfort. A friend of Debbie's who was a part-time pastor delivered a eulogy. Several people shared stories about Moet, which was just what Debbie needed right now. She needed open arms to say, "We're hurting, too, for this little girl that was so special."

Debbie had brought toys, flowers, clothes, notes and many other special items to put around Moet's casket. Moet looked beautiful as she lay in her special blanket, surrounded by so many items that told of her life here on earth. She was peaceful, and the physical demons that had plagued her during her sickness had disappeared. But her mommy's heart was another story; I could see it was in a thousand pieces.

As Debbie's friends and family came into the service, they were each given a folder bearing a beautiful portrait of Moet. The folder contained the service layout and a touching eulogy on Moet's life. They were also given pieces of paper to record their favorite memories of Moet. These were added to a scrapbook that honored Moet.

Moet lay in state at the front of the chapel. She rested comfortably in her favorite blue blanket with paw prints, and had beside her a slew of special items from her life together with her mommy. A gorgeous portrait of Moet, her favorite bone, embroidered with her persona – "bitch" – a special treat, her bright pink collar and leash, a special storybook that she and Debbie would read together, a photo album, flowers from friends and family, candles, and many items were on a table. Everyone who saw this understood what made Moet so special.

There were approximately 30 people in attendance, from Debbie's mom and stepdad, to friends, to co-workers, to Moet's nanny. All of them came with their own emotions as they honored this special little doggie. The grief was almost overwhelming, and each person felt it for his or her own unique reasons. "None of us had ever been to a pet funeral per se," Debbie told me later. "I did a little eulogy, we read poems . . . it was just very comforting. I think it helped everyone." Hugs were also exchanged, and tears were shed. Moet was quite the personality, and she truly had touched many people.

After the service, Debbie's friends and family members lingered at the center. I spent my time circulating throughout the room, giving my condolences, exchanging hugs, and listening to more stories about Moet. People spent time writing down more memories for Debbie, and they also spent more time with Moet's body, stroking her head and giving her kisses on her soft white hair.

Debbie too was lingering, not wanting to leave, as she knew that it would be the last time that she would see her amazing little girl. That last goodbye, that walk out my door, it would take all of the strength that Debbie had remaining.

Debbie stayed around after everyone left and spent some alone-time with her baby girl. There was no sense in even talking about what types of memorialization items she was going to want or need for Moet. Debbie was done making decisions and could not possibly think through anything else. As with many pet parents in this situation, it was time for me to do the thinking for her. To remember the Golden Rule and to say, "What would I want if I were Debbie?"

Answering that question would allow me to take the lead in this area and to be positioned to guide Debbie when she was physically ready.

A Journey of Grief

Debbie still resents the fact that her options were not explained to her as soon as Moet became ill. "I just don't think people are aware of the options out there, and I wanted to be able to treat Moet with respect and dignity," she said. "I think different things work with different people, but I don't think that veterinarians spend much time with their clients." She added, "Anybody

I know who has a pet, I have made them aware of the options. I even went in to my primary veterinarian and talked to him candidly about options and how having a service helped me."

Later, Debbie would change veterinarians, partly because of how she felt Moet's death was handled. "When I went back to talk to him and tell him about what had happened, and how I thought he needed to tell people about these types of wonderful services, he was very compassionate and had tears in his eyes," she said. "But when my neighbor used him about a month later, it was not even brought up, so he obviously did not follow up on what I told him."

After the service, Debbie still would show up at the center, occasionally landing in a heap in my arms. She didn't come to me to find answers to anything or because she needed something in particular. Instead, she came because she knew it was a safe place to cry, to be angry, and to deeply grieve and mourn the loss of Moet. Throughout her journey of grief, I was there to walk beside her as she tried to find answers that were elusive.

It wasn't my journey to take. But as a companion to her, I was there beside her, and together we discovered how she could best deal with her grief. I was humbled to be given the privilege to be there beside her as we continued to honor the story and the life that she shared with Moet.

Debbie also came to the center to visit Moet, whose remains were still at the center in an urn. The reason that Debbie wanted to have Moet cremated was so that she could always have her by her side. If Debbie moved, she did not want to leave Moet behind. Wherever she chose to live would not be complete without the spirit of Moet. Therefore, I was a little surprised when she did not take the urn with Moet's cremated remains back to her home as soon as it was ready. Debbie just needed more time.

The top of the wood urn had an exquisite design of brass and copper flowers. The side of the box had a nameplate, eloquently scripted with Moet's name. It was stunning. But even after months passed, the urn was still at the center. Debbie and I still spent many hours together, crying, sharing, remembering, and just honoring Moet's story. But the thought of bringing the urn home was still too much for her to fathom. Throughout the year, I would occasionally hear my front doorbell ring at the center, walk out and see Debbie, talking sweetly to Moet's urn on the mantle. She would see me, give me a look that said, "I just need some quiet time with My Girl," and I would turn around and leave them alone with their conversation.

Another year passed, and Debbie's grief journey continued. The tears still came, albeit less frequently now, but they were never too far from the surface when she saw me. I had that effect with some families – a vivid reminder that I was the last one to see their special fur baby. I was okay with that as I knew those tears were bittersweet – bitter in the fact that they missed their love and sweet in the fact that they knew someone cared for these little pets even after they died.

Finally, on the second anniversary of Moet's death, Debbie felt strong enough to take her girl home. It was an incredibly moving event as we sat and talked and shared stories. When Debbie decided she was ready to go, I watched her pick up Moet's urn. She was vulnerable again, but she found the courage to quietly walk out the door.

As with every pet parent who has loved, Moet is never far from Debbie's heart and mind. However, my heart was warmed when three years later after Moet died, Debbie was ready to allow herself to love again, to open her heart and to welcome another dog into her life. She walked back into my center with Chloe in her arms. Her new dog was dressed in the finest of clothes with the cutest little bows on her ears, and I knew the circle of life had started all over again. Yes, Moet was never far from her heart, but there was room for another little being to begin residing there, too. Not to replace Moet but to be another love in Debbie's life.

A Letter to Debbie from Coleen Ellis

Dear Debbie:

I'll never forget the look of shock and grief on your face the day I met you. But I'm glad that I remember that look. It reminds me of the utter rawness that one goes through when he or she loses a special pet that is part of the family.

I want to thank you for being the first person who gave me the privilege of doing a full funeral service for their pet. And, a spectacular event it was! It was everything that a little doggie with a name like "Moet" should deserve.

Everyone who came to Moet's funeral came out of respect and love for her and you. However, like most people, I know that there were thoughts of "I wonder what a funeral for a dog is going to look like? Feel like?" As with many people, they had no idea of what to expect.

But, I can tell you one thing – I do know that when people left Moet's service, I heard comments like, "Wow – I hope my funeral is as beautiful as that was!" It truly was the most beautiful tribute to a life well loved – and a gorgeous little Bichon girl who was loved immensely.

The readings were touching and poignant. The memory table that you created, complete with her favorite blanket, toy, leash, collar, and many other snippets of the life that you shared together was amazing. And the hundreds of photos were deeply moving.

What also warmed my heart were the slips of paper that we handed out to the guests, asking them to record a favorite memory they had of Moet. I watched people put their heart into these writings – wanting to capture just the right words for you and for her. I know that you still cherish those writings to this day.

Thanks for giving us me the opportunity to honor Moet's story and to catch a glimpse of the love that you and her shared. I know you still hold that love near and dear to your heart to this day.

Thanks, too, for allowing your heart to love again and for rescuing Chloe. I know that Moet would be proud.

Warm regards,
Coleen

CHAPTER 9

New Players on Grieving the Loss of a Pet

The Loyal and True Pet Cremation Services operation, a division of the Robert D. Loose Funeral Home & Crematory in Anderson, Ind., provides phenomenal services to their local pet parents, mimicking their high touch, caring services they provide to their human families.

Mico was Mommy's Little Girl. I doted on her and treated her just like other mothers treat their human children. She got the best of everything – from veterinary care to toys to clothes. Nothing was too good for her – and she was spoiled rotten. Yes, she was my child.

Therefore, when Mico died, and my options were so few, I grasped for what I could to help me honor her the way that I wanted to. When we were presented with the "option" at the veterinary clinic of putting her precious body in a bag and in a freezer for a route truck to pick up, I knew this was not what was going to happen to my incredible little girl. Coming from the funeral industry, I was relieved when I found a local human funeral home that would handle her cremation. I knew how we honored the dead in the human world, and I thought the funeral home was going to handle my precious little girl and my broken heart with dignity.

But this didn't turn out to be the case. I was devastated when I, once again, ran into indifference regarding how much this loss affected me. I was quickly presented not with caring service but with a business attitude that refused to pay tribute to all the great times we spent together.

First of all, the staff members at the funeral home asked us to use the back door when we arrived as they were "busy." Chris and I took Mico in with us, wrapped in her little blue blanket and with her special toy. We politely asked if we could sit in their chapel for one last moment together, our last time of seeing her beautiful scruffy little body. It was clear that the funeral director was very concerned that no other families should see me because it might make them feel bad if they knew that his business also served families who had lost pet family members. After all, he told me, other families were dealing with a "real" death. He made it sound as though I were lucky that this was all I had to deal with.

In fact, when he did tell us that it was "OK" if we sat in chapel with her, he also asked that we sit in the back of the chapel and not turn on the lights so as not to attract the attention of the other families. So we sat there in the dark, hiding, with my little girl on my lap, holding onto every second that we could with her. It was the last time I got to see her physical body – that body of the special dog who had given me so much joy the past 14 years.

To this day, I wish I had told the funeral director what I had thought about how he was treating me, and of course, how he was treating Mico. At the time, I felt his behavior was shameful, but in my grief, I couldn't even fathom having that type of discussion with him. It just seemed too disrespectful to Mico when this time was clearly all about her. Someday, I would be able to tell my story about this behavior and what it did to affect me for the rest of my life.

The experience broke my heart. The idea that pet parents needed a safe place to grieve and service providers who would respect and help guide them through a difficult time of loss was beginning to take hold in me even then.

Funeral Homes Get Involved

So far, we've focused mostly on veterinarians, pet cemeteries and other businesses that tend to operate separately from what we traditionally think of as death-care operations. However, there are a growing number of human funeral homes that are beginning to realize that families want and need someone to take care of their beloved pets.

Despite my experience with Mico, it's great to see more funeral homes answering the call to fill this void, because they have specialized training in helping people dealing with loss. If they choose to use this training wisely, they have the resources and knowledge to serve pet parents well.

Even if you do not work directly with a funeral home, one may be handling the cremation of your pet if it has an arrangement with your veterinarian. You may also come in contact with a funeral home and funeral directors if you want the body of your pet buried because many funeral homes also own and operate cemeteries. Some of these cemeteries have pet sections or pet-and-human sections. Depending on the law in your state, you may even opt to be buried right alongside your pet or pets in a beautiful setting. This can be a great option because while many pet cemeteries are run efficiently and properly, we've already seen that they may not always be permanent. The states tend to govern human cemeteries more closely, and this is a good thing for pet parents that want to ensure their beloved pets always rest in peace.

Since starting Two Hearts Pet Loss Center, I've had the pleasure of helping many funeral homes start or improve pet death-care operations that truly honor the bond that pet owners share with their pets.

Working with Funeral Homes

As with any pet loss business, do your homework ahead of time to find a pet loss business that you will be comfortable turning to in your time of loss. By asking the right questions, you can make sure to have as peaceful of an experience in honoring your pet as you deserve. By knowing ahead of time what you want to do to honor your pet in death, you will be able to choose a pet loss business that will most clearly resemble your philosophies.

Associations like the International Cemetery, Cremation and Funeral Association have actually begun specific groups to help funeral homes, pet memorial centers, pet cemeteries and pet crematories, and others allied to death care to set standards and help them do better. When I went to the leaders at ICCFA asking if they would consider starting such a group, they knew that something needed to be done to ensure that their member firms would continue to maintain the goodwill that they had worked so hard to build in their respective communities.

Today, I have the pleasure of leading their Pet Loss Professionals Alliance, which regularly holds meetings to talk about best practices and standards within our industry. We also strive to provide educational opportunities so the pet loss professional you are working with is very well versed and trained in this area.

There are other death-care associations that are also available to pet loss operations. The International Association of Pet Cemeteries has been around for quite some time and recently moved to new offices in Atlanta. The group also recently announced a partnership with the Cremation Association of North America to continue to educate their members on best practices and raise the level of standards for their members.

The Pet Loss Industry Sees a Change

As a noted leader in the field of pet loss, pet grief, and pet funeral home consulting, I've had the experience of meeting many funeral directors who treat their pet families the way I wish I had been treated when I lost Mico. From Florida to California, Texas to Canada, so many wonderful people have crossed my path with the same mission as mine – to provide dignified and respectful death care services to beloved pets. Many of these people have had a less than stellar experience with the loss of their precious pet that subsequently a business was born out of the need to make sure that it was done differently for other pet parents.

Kevin and Joanna Woronchak had a horrific experience with the loss of three beloved pets, a short time apart from each other. Therefore, Until We Meet Again Pet Memorial Services was born in Vancouver, Canada. Ross DeJohn and brother, Bob, can both eloquently and emotionally recall two special pets and the uncaring experiences they encountered when these animals died. They are now serving families in the Cleveland area at the family's operation, DeJohn Pet Services. And, Cay Dalrymple saw the need for respectful pet death-care services in the Houston area after she watched what her doggie kennel customers went through when their precious pets died. Therefore, Paws Memorial Service was born to provide another option to caring pet parents in that market.

There are countless other stories like this in the pet loss industry. These stories include incredibly respectful pets-only types of pet memorialization companies as well as human funeral homes now beginning to include pet memorialization services. Stories where individuals have said, "I didn't like how that process happened to me when my pet died so I'm going to make sure it doesn't happen to anyone else" or businesses that have said, "Pet parents are wanting more in the options available to them when their pet dies – let's give them what they need." As a pet parent, I am grateful for those that are starting these services and allowing us the opportunity to know there are options and the support to validate our grief journey.

For my human funeral home colleagues, having the privilege to serve pet parents is a true gift to them. As pet loss professionals, guiding a family through the loss of a special pet will, many times, be an educational event for everyone involved. We as death-care professionals are proud to be caregivers, to be guides and to be a resource.

As my colleague, John McQueen of Pet Passages in Tampa, Fla., said, "Since many individuals only experience intimately the death of a loved one perhaps twice in one's life, the majority of individuals are less and less familiar with death and the need for ceremony." He added, "However, during that same lifetime, imagine how many pets a family will own." Families should be given the same dignity and respect when a pet dies as when human family members die.

Like many of my colleagues, I know that the demand for pet memorialization options will only increase as time goes on. As the dynamics of the family unit continue to change, for more and more families, their pets are their family. As many baby boomers are empty-nesting, the pets are becoming the new children. And, while they will want them treated like little people in life, they will certainly want them treated the same way in death. Furthermore, more and more young families are waiting to have children. Again the pets are becoming their surrogate children.

What Other Professionals are Saying

One of the first businesses I consulted with in the startup of their pet funeral division was the Hillcrest-Flynn Pet Funeral Home and Crematory in Hermitage, Pa. The Flynns had an existing human funeral home and cemetery, but they have built one of the finest pet funeral operations in the United States.

When the business opened in November 2006, I was proud to train Roberta Knauf, a pet funeral director at the Flynn operation. Tom Flynn, the owner of Hillcrest Memorial Park, the cemetery next to the new pet funeral home, was the proud pet parent of Derek, a golden retriever that did work for him as a pet therapy dog for the John Flynn Funeral Home and Crematory. Whenever you saw Tom, you'd see Derek at his side. Roberta herself came from the pet industry – operating a pet store in the local area as well as being a certified dog trainer. She was also one of the founding members of the Pennsylvania Prison Puppy Program.

"The response not only from the pet people but the general public has been 100 percent positive," Roberta said. "We felt it important to do our research before we started the business – and because we took this extra time to reach out to others that have pet loss businesses, we've been incredibly happy with what we offer our pet parent families."

I love talking to Roberta and sharing stories of those families she's working with. In fact, I could talk for hours with others that are guiding families through this very difficult time. One of the things that I learned early on is that the loss of a pet may have many of the same attributes as the loss of a human family member. However, there are some differences, too. For instance, with the death of a pet, the feelings and emotions are those of merely love and grief. A pet does not have a will to read, an estate to divide, nor baggage in the form of hurt feelings to bring to the final arrangements from days gone past. No, with a pet, it's pure love and pure grief. It's so beautiful to be a part of it all.

Anyway, after only a few years in business, Roberta already has many fond memories of the families she's helped. "I had a family come in to purchase a pet lot for their 13-year-old dog in our pet cemetery," she said. "The family consisted of a single mother, 9-year-old daughter named Lindy and an elderly grandmother."

The mother explained to Roberta that her daughter had never experienced a death, and she knew that when their lab mix, Lady, died, it was going to be extremely hard on everyone. "She wanted to be prepared," Roberta said. "About three weeks later, I received a call from Barb stating that her daughter's guinea pig died. 'I don't know what to do, can you help me?' she said. 'Do you cremate guinea pigs?' she asked. I replied, 'Yes we do, but Barb you have a cemetery lot here. Why don't we bury Squeaky there?' She asked, 'We can do that? Can my daughter come up and be there? Will you be there to help us?' My reply was 'yes' to all. Lindy came in with her mom, and we talked about what she would like to have at the service for the guinea pig, named Squeaky. She wanted her best friend to come, have flowers, and I asked her to write a story about Squeaky."

Roberta shared with me that the service that followed in the pet cemetery was very touching. "Lindy's grandmother took me aside and thanked me for opening the discussion about death and dying," Roberta said. "You see, she was diagnosed with cancer and did not know how to start a conversation with her granddaughter. I truly believe that if we show children how to memorialize their pets they will have a better understanding of death all around."

Roberta hopes other pet loss professionals will make themselves available to provide these services for pet parents. "We are so grateful to our veterinarians to heal and prevent the death of our precious pets," she said. "Therefore, educating those that are in the medical industry on what the options are for pet parents when death does happen is so important. For the medical industry, it's much like the same process that they use when they refer a client to another type of medical specialist for treatment processes that they themselves don't specialize in. For a pet loss professional, we are that specialist, it just happens to be in death. Furthermore, much like our human funeral homes . . . when a person dies at the hospital, the doctor does not then play funeral director. The family is sent to the next professional, the funeral director, to then begin the process of the final arrangements."

She went on, "Also, much like we have the opportunity to preplan our final arrangements as human beings, families should also be given the appropriate literature to help the client prepare for the day." She added, "I want to see more pet funeral homes start up – whether private and stand-alone or in conjunction with a human funeral home. The more of us that are out there, the more the public will know that there are options when it comes to respectful and dignified pet death-care services."

As another human funeral home colleague, Dan Isard with The Foresight Companies in Phoenix, stated, "People have memories with their pets. Many people make arrangements to be buried or interred with their pet's cremated remains." He added, "Constructive mourning is beneficial to us as a society. We can teach a child to mourn and grieve using the life of a pet as a teacher."

Celebrants Also Step in to Play a Role

As I began to do my research for what is happening in the pet loss industry, I uncovered the work of celebrants. Many people already use celebrants for wedding ceremonies and other special events. Celebrants have also begun helping families celebrate the lives of loved ones. Although they mainly deal with humans, they are also increasingly involved with helping families remember pets that were considered part of the family.

Risa Marlen, a life cycle celebrant with Healing Heart Ceremonies in New Jersey, is getting more inquiries about families wanting to hold ceremonies for beloved pets. She is also a psychotherapist, and she first thought about holding a service for a pet after discovering that a client's dog had been run over. "The family was filled with guilt and anger," she said. "I shared that I am also a life cycle celebrant and offered to conduct a pet memorial at their home."

Risa did not expect the family to take her up on the offer, but they did. "It was my first one," she shared. "When I saw firsthand how meaningful and sacred the ceremony was for the participants, I knew that this was a service that I felt blessed to be able to offer."

The service was so meaningful because family members of all ages participated. "They were given the opportunity to come forward and express their thoughts at the urn," she said. "Some had written things; others spoke directly from the heart. But what was most moving was that a family that was initially divided along lines of guilt and anger was now unified in a sense of shared grieving."

Risa has witnessed firsthand how much pets can mean to their owners, and she thinks holding services to honor that shared relationship is supremely worthwhile. "It honors the fact that animal companions truly do become members of our families, and as such, when they pass away they are sorely missed," she said. "Formally memorializing this sends a message to adults that they do not need to feel foolish that their hearts may feel broken. For children, pet loss is often their very first encounter with death. A pet memorial can provide the template for the child to begin to come to terms with this rite of passage."

Pet celebrants are just one more resource to help families pay tribute to the life that was lived and shared together.

Despite how important pets are to people, Risa says that many people still don't know about pet memorial services. "But once presented, almost everyone responds with something to the effect of, 'Boy, I really could have used this service a while back!' or, 'I know someone who recently lost a pet, and could really use your help!' In sum, the need is there. The challenge is in getting the word out."

Pet parents need professional pet loss providers to help guide them through their loss. The bottom line is that there are a number of options for pet parents to explore. From selecting the pet loss operation that's right for you – a stand-alone pet funeral home, a pet cremation service, a pet cemetery, a human funeral home with pet loss services – to deciding on the professionals to guide you – from a celebrant to a certified pet loss professional – it's important to know who you are dealing with. You also must be comfortable that they will honor the relationship and treat your pet's remains with respect and dignity.

CHAPTER 10

A Tribute to Cherokee

I've always enjoyed working with children, but I must admit it can be tough helping them cope with the loss of a beloved pet. A child's innocence, love and individual personality are all ingredients that allow me to create a rich experience when it comes to their grief journey. However, the main ingredient in this experience is the permission that their parents will give them to do what they need to do to show their grief and to mourn in the way that is appropriate for them.

When an entire family is involved in mourning a precious pet, however, it is challenging to explain the process and get everyone involved. There can be incredible amounts of emotion, as each family member grieves in his or her own way.

Working with Heather, Steve and Forrest was especially moving. I worked with Heather, the pet mommy, and also guided her son, Forrest, to honor their dog, Cherokee. I needed to help each of them grieve in a way that was important to them. The family will forever stay in my heart because of how they allowed themselves to perform the rituals necessary for their family to honor their big love.

I also worked with the pet daddy, Steve, who initially notified me of Cherokee's death. With that first phone call from him, I knew from his tone of voice what had happened. His voice was laced with sadness and grief – as well as a forced tone of control. It was a tone of voice I've had from many pet dads – they hated to cry on the phone, but the tears were always right there at the surface. Handling their phone calls is always interesting. I needed to respect their vulnerability but also make sure I covered all the bases regarding the initial arrangements for their pet. And I needed to be sure I was emotionally there for the rest of the family, too.

The Terrible Discovery

When Steve got home from work, he let Cherokee, their beautiful St. Bernard, outside to do her bathroom duties. When she did not come back to be let in, he went to check on her. She was lying on her side in the yard. Clearly, she had died.

The call from Steve was wrought with confusion and questions. Cherokee was "mommy's girl," and Mommy was on her way home from work. They had an 8-year old son, Forrest, who loved his "sister" and was now facing his first experience with death. Steve was trying to figure out how to manage all of these moving parts as well as his own emotions of the loss of his pretty girl and the loss of his love, too.

I found out when I arrived at the house that word of Cherokee's death had already begun to spread throughout the neighborhood. Neighbors came out of their homes to make their way to the Pope/Rock household to see what they could do to help and also to say their goodbyes to Cherokee.

Steve instinctively wanted me to take Cherokee so that his family did not have to see their big girl "like this." I told Steve that I would be there as support, and I emphasized that it was important for everyone to get the chance to see Cherokee one last time, to hug her for the last time, to give her a kiss on her beautiful head and to prepare themselves emotionally to say their goodbyes.

This was going to be a significant part of the process. The family certainly needed this time, to back up and say "hello," to remember all that Cherokee had brought to the family, and to begin to prepare themselves for their individual grief journeys. As I watched each one of them pay their respects, I realized that each one of them was going back into time to when Cherokee came home as a bundle of puppy joy, the Christmases, the Halloweens, the first time that she met her human brother, Forrest, and the numerous other special events along the way.

An Entire Community Mourns

As an observer of this process, it played out as I had seen it numerous times before. The neighbors gathered around and began to tell stories about Cherokee. There were funny times, special events and other memories that came crashing through. It seemed like people told stories for hours, but it really wasn't that long. It was incredibly touching to watch this support system kick in for the family and to listen to so many people pay their tributes to this stoic girl.

When Heather pulled into the driveway and got out of her vehicle, Steve met her with a hug and the tears began. Together, they made their way to the backyard to Cherokee's body. I heard the cries, even louder. Once again, I was reduced to tears as well.

As the family dealt with their tremendous loss, I began to determine what I must do to help each of them through their individual grief journeys. Heather's world had clearly been rocked. Her maternal instincts kicked in as Cherokee had joined the family even before her son. Steve, meanwhile, wrestled with his own emotions as he tried to muster the strength to take care of his wife and his son. I turned my attention to Forrest as Heather and Steve dealt with their emotions.

Feelings of Guilt

The days and the follow up with Heather were intense. She was full of questions. She kept asking herself "why?" Had she missed something in Cherokee's health that she should've seen? Why did this happen now? And, the question that grieving pet parents always seem to bring up at this moment: *Will I ever be able to love another pet like I loved this one?*

None of these questions really needed immediate answers. I spent my time with Heather trying to guide her through the grief journey, and we developed a close relationship and remain friends to this day. Sometimes, I just listened. Sometimes I talked. However, every time I let Heather lead the way, and I was just there to walk alongside her.

When she was ready, Heather decided that she wanted to do something special for Cherokee. She wanted to have her version of a memorial service, and she turned to me for help and guidance. I knew that I had just been delivered an incredible opportunity to guide her and her family in setting up this service that would be fit for a queen. After all, that is truly what Cherokee was in their house.

However, there was also another part of this process. Forrest wanted to do something to personally pay tribute to Cherokee, and after a great deal of thought, we concluded that a donation drive to benefit the local Humane Society would be the perfect thing to do. So, the plans were put into place! Forrest would lead the drive to honor Cherokee, and we would also make the drive a part of the service. This would be a way for everyone that loved Cherokee to give to the other animals that did not get to have the wonderfully spoiled life that she had.

Preparing for the Service

The invitations for the Celebration of Life were created, the posters were made for Forrest to distribute, the guest list was developed, and the celebration fit for a queen was put into play.

Forrest distributed the Memorial Fund Drive posters throughout the neighborhood as well as at his school. I loaned him a large wicker dog bed to collect his donations at school. The poster was not only beautiful – it was one of the most touching pieces I have ever seen. His message to the world about honoring his wonderful dog, Cherokee, was priceless. I was so proud of him and what he wanted to do for her.

Forrest's drive continued – and I received progress reports constantly! The dog bed had to be emptied into their garage a few times – to make room for more items! People were so respectful of Forrest and what he wanted to do to honor his dog.

Heather did a beautiful job creating the invitation to the Celebration of Life event, which included a list of items that the Humane Society needed and a slip of paper to share a memory of Cherokee. Everyone brought items to donate and their recorded memories to the service.

I was honored to be included in a service that was all about the love that an animal brings to a family. I knew that it would be emotional, but I was ready to drink in the love and the caring.

The Celebration of Life was on a Friday night. My mom happened to be in town, and she joined me at the service. As an animal lover, she was delighted to be with others that loved animals, too. She wanted to see how everyone honored this special girl.

As people walked into the door, they were asked for their donation item for the Humane Society drive. They were still doing all that they could to give back in Cherokee's honor!

On the computer in the living room was a screensaver that showed photos of Cherokee enjoying life with his family. As people made their way into the kitchen, they came across a spread of food Heather had prepared. All of the dishes had some special meaning to Cherokee. There was the human food that Cherokee enjoyed such as deviled eggs, popcorn and pretzels. I was most impressed with the bowl of dark brown crunchy bread pieces, taken out of the bags and bags of Tasty Mix treats. Heather and Steve had painstakingly gone through numerous bags to extract just this piece as it was Cherokee's favorite ingredient in the bag. The spread was completed with cupcakes adorned with paw prints and one of my favorites, "puppy chow," a delicious mixture of Chex cereal with chocolate, peanut butter and powdered sugar topping.

Heather had also put up a tribute table for Cherokee. There were numerous items that were special: Cherokee's urn, her paw print, her fur clipping and the scrapbook that Heather was putting together for her. It was here that I dropped off my slip of paper with my memory. Even though I never knew Cherokee when she was living, I could easily tell how much this dog was loved, and that's what I wrote about on the slip of paper.

Sharing Fellowship and Finding a New Pet

As the open-house style service continued, we enjoyed listening to stories about Cherokee. At one point in the evening, Steve asked me to say a few words about the importance of having a service for this precious pet. Again, my heart was so warm with love and honor for this wonderful dog.

The night came to an end, and the grief journey continued. Heather had an incredibly difficult time as she actively mourned Cherokee. We spent hours together, honoring Cherokee's story and letting Heather talk, cry, get angry – whatever it was she needed.

As time went on, Heather's heart began to heal from her loss. She also began to believe that, once again, she was ready to allow herself to love another dog again. It just so happened, that at this same time we knew of a St. Bernard that had been left homeless. I gingerly made the phone call to Heather, inquiring as to her interest in meeting Addy.

The first meeting was incredibly emotional with thoughts of "Am I cheating on Cherokee?" to "She's not like Cherokee." However, after Addy met the entire family, Heather decided that this new St. Bernard would join their home.

It's been an interesting journey with this family and Addy, who has been certified as a service dog. Addy and Heather spend many hours in schools helping children learn how to read through the Paws and Read program. I think this is an incredible tribute to Cherokee and a way to give back to the community.

A Special Letter

So many times, we wish we knew what our pets are thinking. Many years ago, I found this letter that I think sums up what our pets would say to us after they die:

My Dear Family,

To have loved and then said farewell, is better than to have never loved at all.

For all of the times that you have stopped and touched my head, fed me my favorite treat and returned the love that I so unconditionally gave to you. For the care that you gave to me so unselfishly. For all of these things I am grateful and thankful.

I ask that you not grieve for the loss but rejoice in the fact that we lived, loved and touched each other's lives. My life was fuller because you were there, not as a master and owner but as my friend.

Today I am as I was in my youth. The grass is always green, butterflies flit among the flowers and the sun shines gently down upon all of God's creatures. I can run, jump, play and do all of the things that I did in my youth. There is no sickness, no aching joints and no regrets and no aging.

We await the arrival of our lifelong companions and know that togetherness is forever. You live in our hearts as we do in yours. Companions such as you are so rare and unique. Don't hold the love that you have within yourself. Give it to another like me and then I will live forever. For love never really dies and you are loved and missed as surely as we are.

It is natural for people to think about whether they can love another pet when grieving a tremendous loss. Well-meaning people think that if they get another pet, the pain will be diminished or go away. For a grieving heart, it's an individual decision on when, if at all, the time is right to love another pet. But, as the above letter does state, the opening of a heart and the willingness to love again is a beautiful tribute to a deceased pet in saying "I loved what we shared so much that I want to love another!"

People should not get a new pet to replace the deceased pet but to experience another furry personality. Again, the time frame as to when this is right for a person or a family is an individual decision and one that should not be hurried.

Heather, Steve and Forrest gave again to Addy, and they also added another dog, Quincy. This doesn't change the fact that they will always remember all the great times they had with Cherokee.

Dogs Need Items!

Hi my name is FORREST. I am in 3rd grade. Our dog (Cherokee) has passed away. I want to help other dogs. I want to get stuff for the dogs that don't have owners. Can you please donate dog stuff for the Humane Society? Please put your donation in the box. I will take the stuff to the Humane Society and make a donation in Cherokee's memory.

THANK YOU for any help you can give.

Forrest

Indianapolis Humane Society Donation Suggestions

bath/hand towels (no holes)
blankets (no holes or electric blankets)
comforters (no holes)

soft dog treats
rawhide bones and chews

Kongs (all sizes)
treat dispensing toys
Nylabones
puppy toys

bleach
paper towel rolls

spray bottles
trash bags
dust pans w/brushes
rubber gloves

stainless food bowls
dog crates
pet shampoo
pooper scoopers

gift certificates from stores that sell
pet items
checks made out to Indianapolis Humane
Society

CHAPTER 11

Honoring a K-9 Officer Who Served with Honor

Above, the stage is set to honor Bo and his amazing work with the Indianapolis Metropolitan Police Department.

I had just picked up a precious little Shih-Tzu named "Norman Rockwell" that had belonged to police Sgt. William Berger with the Indianapolis Metropolitan Police Department.

As I drove, I was thinking about how creative people can get in naming their pets. "Norman Rockwell" was even cuter than I could have imagined, and when I arrived at my center, I placed a call to Sgt. Berger to let him know that his Norman was safe with me. When I got him on the phone, however, I could immediately tell that something else was wrong.

He said, "Coleen, not one minute before you called me, I just heard on the scanner that we just lost a police dog in pursuit. Lt. Benny Diggs and the department need you right now to help with this dog that just got shot. Please call him."

My heart sank as I realized that a four-legged officer lost his life doing his job. I also knew that this wasn't the first time that the department had to cope with such a loss. In September 2006, a police dog named Arco was shot and killed in the line of duty. At that time, I had the honor of serving the Indianapolis Metropolitan Police Department during a very tough time, and as sad as I was to hear the news that another dog had died in the line of duty, I was ready to help in any way I could.

I picked up the phone and called Benny, commander of the department's canine unit, and he picked up almost as soon as it started ringing.

"Benny, I was on the phone with one of your guys, and he heard what happened on his scanner. What's going on?" I asked.

"We lost one today, Coleen," he said. "It's Bo. Officer Johnson is OK, but Bo took the bullet for him. We were in pursuit, and the guy just turned and shot him. We're going to need you, Coleen, but I have to go be with our police officers right now."

"I'm here for you, Benny. Call me when you can," I said.

I immediately put the team on notice that we were going to be assisting with another canine police officer. I had conducted another such service two years earlier, so I knew what the department wanted and how it liked to operate in setting up these services. I waited to hear from Benny.

Recalling Arco's Service

As I waited to hear more details, I thought about the last police dog service I had handled for the Indianapolis Police Department. In 2006, Arco was shot and killed in the line of duty. I had reached out to Lt. Diggs after hearing about Arco's death, and the first thing he told me was that he wanted to be sure that Arco's handler would want a memorial service.

While Benny hadn't specifically sought out my services, he was pleased to get my phone call offering help. "I always kind of felt we never recognized these dogs' heroics as much as we should have," he said. "Dogs also die in the line of duty. And although we had some things done for these dogs, it was nothing like the real memorial service that we held for Arco," he told me later.

Arco's handler, Officer Mark Archer, was grieving deeply for his lost partner, as was his family and the entire force. Arco had taken a bullet in the head to protect his handler. Several officers asked me on more than one occasion: "What more can you ask of your partner than that?"

When I handled Arco's services, I felt as though I were engaged in a bit of a courtship. I was trying to get to know the department and Benny, and he was trying to get to know me. We worked together to ensure we created a service that respected Arco as a K-9 officer without disrespecting human officers and their importance in protecting the community. I did my best to honor the wishes of the department, but I also found that the officers in charge didn't really know what they wanted because this was the first service of its kind that they had ever overseen.

I learned from them and followed their lead in areas where they had ideas, and then guided them in areas where I knew what needed to be done. This was certainly a learning experience for me – and I knew that, heaven forbid, if I had to do this again, I would do a better job leading them. I made sure to take copious notes along the way so that I'd be duly prepared if my services were needed again. I hoped this wouldn't be the case, but I wanted to be prepared nonetheless.

One of the great things we did at Arco's service is that we honored two other K-9 dogs that had earlier been killed in the line of duty. As people walked in to honor Arco, they passed a table that had photos of all the dogs that had been killed along with plaques and candles that honored their service. Benny commented to me on more than one occasion that it was interesting how the handlers of these dogs were still "not over" the deaths of their K-9 partners, even all these years later.

Planning the service as well as being there for Officer Archer and his family took up the days leading up to the memorial. People across the city were intrigued by this service, and every news station in town was ready to bring the trucks.

The day of the service rolled around. I had made sure the participants were ready, the color guard in line, the honor guard prepared, and that the community had come out to show their support. Still, I was a nervous wreck because I was afraid I'd missed a detail somewhere.

The service was amazing, filled with eulogies, readings, tears, and much emotion. After the service, much like any other funeral service, members of the Marion County Sherriff's Department shared an intimate dinner, giving themselves time as a department to come together for support and to share their own stories of Arco.

Officers and Their Dogs Share a Strong Bond

I knew from previous conversations with Benny that he believes honoring these dogs not only helps the officers that work with them but also members of the community that they protect. "When you harm an animal, especially a service animal, people become very upset," he said. "A memorial service brings closure to the whole incident and the violent death that a dog had. It brings closure to the occurrence and makes everyone feel a little better."

I'd gotten to know Benny well during the time he and his fellow officers dealt with Arco's loss. He is now working with his fourth police dog that is due to retire soon. I'd spoken with him at length about the bonds that officers share with their dogs. "They are in the car with you every night, and you find yourself talking to them," Benny told me. "Anytime you spend seven or eight hours a day with a person or dog, you develop a pretty significant bond."

All of Benny's dogs have died because of old age, but losing a dog is always hard, he said. "I think the toughest one was my first patrol dog," he told me. "He lived to be 10, and I replaced him when he was 8. He was probably the dog that was closest to me, and I remember when he passed away that he couldn't get up and walk or anything like that; we had to have the veterinarian come to the house and give him a shot to put him out of his misery. Sometimes, you question whether or not you waited too long to do the inevitable because you don't want them to pass away."

Benny said he thinks many officers develop their strongest bond with their first dog. Each officer chooses to handle his or her dog's death in their own way. "There is an area here in Indiana where they will take the dog's remains, and all of my dogs have been sent there," he said. "I haven't kept the remains in urns or anything like that, but that is just me and just the way I like to do things. But some officers would prefer to keep their dog's ashes where they can see them on a daily basis."

Typically, a police officer will get a service dog around age 2, and the dog will be kept in service eight years or so. "You spend more time with these dogs than anyone else," Benny confided. "I just think you get so involved with them that you want to be sure that when they pass away, you can remember them. You will always remember them in your heart, and I have pictures of all my dogs."

Bo's Heroics

I would later learn from Officer Scott Johnson, Bo's police dog handler, just how heroic his canine partner was when he met a deadly criminal May 10, 2007. Bo, a big German shepherd, was chasing burglars when he was shot and killed.

"I was kind of running with the dog when I could tell he locked onto the bad guy," Scott told me. "The guy was 75 yards or so ahead of Bo, and I saw both suspects disappear. I heard a couple of gunshots, and then I see this guy standing there after coming around the corner; he was standing up and pointing his gun at the dog. I holler, and he points the gun at me."

Scott paused and continued: "Bo is still alive at this point, and the guy takes off running, and Bo still keeps chasing him. I can tell obviously something is wrong because he's not catching the suspect. So we run down the street, and the suspect turns again to try to shoot. I shoot him and hit him at the end of the street. Bo is still chasing him, and the bad guy tosses his gun and falls to the ground. I call Bo to me, and he's gotten really slow. He's coming back to me, and he gets back to me, and he pretty much just falls at my feet."

Tears started to fill my eyes as Scott continued telling me his story. "(The criminal) would have ambushed officers instead of the dog," he said, referring to Bo's heroics. "Bo comes back to me, and he just falls over and is just looking at me. And I'm just looking everywhere, and I knew he was probably shot, but I couldn't tell where. I put my hand underneath him, and I could feel blood, and he's just looking at me. That's the hard part. My wife and I don't have any kids – we had Bo and two other dogs that stayed in the house with me at the time. So I scooped him up and tried to run back to the car with him to try to get to a veterinarian. And then I looked down, and he was already gone."

Scott told me that he had the pleasure of being with Bo for six precious years. "All officers are close to their dogs," he told me. "I know guys who are some of the best policemen and the toughest guys I know who were crying that day, and it's been singlehandedly probably the most life-altering thing I've experienced yet, and I've been a policeman for 16 years. The canine guys spend more time with the dog than their wives. Bo stayed in the house with us, and he'd lie in bed while we were watching TV. He went to work with me every day, and there wasn't much time we spent apart."

Moving Forward

When Benny called me back with details on Bo's service, he agreed that this was one heroic dog. Bo was doing what he was trained to do, what he had done hundreds of times before, in pursuing a criminal. He had a record a mile long of bad guys that he had brought to justice through his tenacity, his strong jaws and his fierce appearance. He was one of the top dogs in the department.

A short amount of time passed before Benny called back. Bo had been taken to the coroner's office. With the K-9s being looked upon as officers, the coroner's office needed to pronounce the death and to rule the cause of death as well. This would be used in court against the criminal. This guy had killed an officer and would face the full force of the law.

Benny also told me that the officers at the site of the shooting had rallied around Scott and Bo to lend their support. As they took Bo to the coroner's department, they took one last ride by the police department.

One last ride for Bo.

One last ride for Officer Johnson and his now deceased partner.

When Benny relayed this story to me, his voice cracked, and I cried.

Waiting and Preparing

It would be a few days before they would release Bo's body as they needed to complete the autopsy. We anxiously awaited the call and began doing what we could to prepare for the upcoming memorial service.

Benny maintained a sense of strength and calm during this very emotional time, and Scott took some time off to mourn his loss. Since Scott and his wife, Kathleen, had no children, Bo and their other four-legged pets, Sasha, Brianna, and Racer, *were* their children. This was going to be a tough loss for the entire family. Kathleen was certainly going to go through her own grief journey and also need to help her husband cope with losing a partner that was with him 24 hours a day.

Scott was never apart from Bo for five years, and when they were away from work, Bo was just like any other member of the family when he was at home. He was such an essential and accepted part of the family unit that he was often found being chased around the house – by the cat! Yes, at home, he was just one of the kids. Oh, this grief journey was going to have many people involved.

I began to think about all the details that would need to be handled, the questions I needed to ask and the phone calls I needed to make. I'd need to order flowers, service folders and take care of other details. Also, I'd need to contact so many people who would want to participate and honor Bo and be there for Scott.

As I continued to think about everything that needed to be done, I flashed back to a conversation I once had with Sgt. Allen Tuttle of the Marion County Sherriff's department. Sgt. Tuttle had been an incredibly valuable resource to us during the first K-9 memorial service that we held for Arco. He had brought things to us that we would need, he called attention to details and he was the go-to guy who made coordinating the service seamless.

After Arco's service, Sgt. Tuttle had stopped by the center to finalize some details for the department. As we were reviewing the service, he said, "You know, Coleen, some people, including myself, were worried about how this service was going to come off – was it going to be weird? Were others going to think it was weird, and ultimately 'cheesy?' We all had a bit of trepidation. But, I have to tell you, from the way that your team handled the crowd, the service, and all of the details of the event, it was the classiest and most caring service that I have been a part of. We as a department were so proud of everything."

I had always remembered that comment as it had made such an impact on me. Now, here we were again, in a position of wanting to make this service as beautiful, as classy and as memorable as the service we had done for Arco. It was such an honor to be helping the police department once again.

Planning the Service

Benny finally called when the coroner was ready to release Bo's body. I sent Brian over to get him and to begin the process of getting Bo ready for cremation so his remains could be returned home to his family.

The next few days were a blur. We made a decision that the service would be on May 31 at a local high school auditorium. Given the number of attendees at Arco's service, we knew we needed to be prepared for a large crowd. Now it was a matter of pulling together all of the details and making sure that not a stone was left unturned for this service.

Being a very detailed person, I still had the notes and information from the last service. As a result, my conversations with Benny were much more succinct and action-oriented as I focused on getting all of the specifics in line. One of our first tasks was to meet with the administration team, Scott and Benny at the Franklin Central High School auditorium to begin the planning process. With the looks of the facility, I knew that we had the right venue for this service. The space was large enough to handle the turnout and accommodating enough to handle the processionals, the bagpiper, the dignitaries, the color guard and the many other officers that would attend.

I began making phone calls to get the various participants in line for the service. As expected, everyone was more than willing to participate, and much like myself, honored to do so. Meanwhile, Brian began to work on finding an appropriate urn for Bo's remains and also began working with a local digital artist to create a portrait. Both pieces turned out just beautiful and were such special works of art. We also began working with Scott and Kathleen to extract Bo from their family photos in order to put together some classy art pieces.

As the day for the service quickly approached, the details were coming together. We were also blessed to have our pet-loving friends call and volunteer their services to assist with the event. Kate Edick and Sandra Braun were such life savers – both darling pet moms that wanted to do their part in making sure the Johnson family and Bo were honored for all that they had done for the community.

All parties were lined up for their specific roles within the service. A retired officer had volunteered to have a dove present at the service, a bagpiper was commissioned and the bugler was ready. Throughout all of these preparations, I made sure to not forget the reason for this tribute – the loss of Bo and the grief journey of his human family, both personally and professionally. I made sure to be there in every way that I could for the department and Officer Johnson and Kathleen.

Honoring Bo

The day arrived for Bo's service, and everything was in place.

As we approached the front of the auditorium, we walked by a classic "fallen officer" unmounted horse, with the officer standing at full attention next to the horse and the boots positioned backwards. A few steps later, we found ourselves next to Scott's patrol car, where he and Bo spent hours upon hours, making the streets safe for everyone in the Marion County area. The car was wrapped in black ribbon, with paw prints adorning the complete band around the vehicle.

Making our way into the auditorium, there were tables full of sympathy cards and notes from people all over the world. The most touching letters, pictures and notes were from the children, who expressed such love, caring and innocence. Peppered among the letters and cards were special items of Bo's, from his harness to his favorite ball from home. The tears began to flow as people looked at the pieces of a life that Bo so selflessly gave to others.

As the attendees made their way into the lobby, there was also a DVD playing that Scott's brother-in-law put together. The footage included Bo in action and photos. There were also newspaper articles on display that recounted Bo's heroic life. The stories focused on how Bo gave his life trying to protect his handler and pursue the bad guys. There was also a table with service folders and a register book. Families took their time as they looked at the cards, watched the DVD and spent time with others.

One particularly poignant moment was when Officer Mark Archer, Arco's handler, made his way through the crowd at the service. It had only been a few short months ago that we had all come together to honor his dog, also killed in the line of duty. Officer Archer quietly and respectfully approached Officer Johnson, offering his sympathies and internally, remembering his grief as well.

The time of the service had come. Forty cadets in training and dignitaries that were in attendance were seated. Then it was time for Brian and me to assemble all of the K-9 officers from throughout the state with their wives. We brought in this group from both sides of the auditorium and sat them together in the center of the room.

The bagpiper was positioned in the rafters of the auditorium, and he began to play Amazing Grace. Brian and I began the processional with the officers, who remained standing for the seating of the officials on the stage, the posting of the colors, and the posting of the honor guard. Being in task mode, I was fully engaged with making sure that everything was going okay. However, when I looked up at the stage and saw the honor guard standing at attention, saluting Bo's portrait, and then ceremoniously cocking their guns, my eyes could no longer hold back the tears.

The service went beautifully. Each one of the speakers and their messages, the music, the soothing and cooing sounds of the dove on the stage and all the other pieces contributed to an incredibly moving ceremony that honored Bo. During the service, a poem about police dogs written by an unknown author was read aloud. I'd like to share it with you:

The Life of a Police Dog

You brought me home
One sunny day
With you for years
I would surely stay.

I met your pack
Children and wife

Coleen Ellis

I began to love
My new-found life.

I slept on your couch
At the foot of your bed
You looked at me lovingly
While petting my head.

We trained for months
And our bonding grew
We were both partners
Buddies in Blue.

We did school demos
And I never did wrong
Over all the years
My love for you grew strong.

How I loved to work
To stand up and bark
In the back of our car
From light until dark.

We went call to call
Having fun all the way
Until the call came
On that one fateful day.

A man with a gun
The dispatcher did say
I jumped from my car
When it pointed your way.

Before leaving home I was told
"Keep him safe" by your wife
I knew at that moment
For you I would give my life.

The bullet struck hard
Steady and true

The bullet struck me instead
Of striking you.

When you go home tonight
Tell your wife I did good
Strong, Tall and Proud
On the ground that I stood.

I'm dead and gone now
This much is true
But I've done my job well
Of protecting you.

Thank you
Loyal partner,
Faithful friend,
You will be greatly missed.

—*Author Unknown*

Many Tears Are Shed

The service concluded with a bugler in the rafters of the auditorium, playing taps. It was a phenomenal conclusion to a service filled with emotion, pride and many tears.

As the service winded down, the officers went to the back, and the rest of the congregation followed. My team spent the next few hours making sure that everyone's needs and requests were handled, and we paid special attention to Kathleen and Scott.

The evening ended, and my team made sure that the building was clean and orderly. It was time to take my team out for a dinner of gratitude for all of their hard work. I know that each of them had poured every bit of energy and emotion into this evening, all to make sure that Bo's life was honored and his death was given every ritual that it deserved.

This service was certainly a small, small token of my appreciation for Officer Scott Johnson, K-9 Officer Bo and all human and K-9 officers for what they do on a daily basis for me and everyone else in my community. My role continues to be to safely hold up their grief, be a companion to them in their grief journeys and help them as needed. I hope that people will one day think of me much like they remember Bo when they read the inscription on his urn – *"Served With Honor."*

In Conclusion

After the service, Benny carefully monitored the community's reaction to Bo's service. "There was one person who wrote a letter to the editor saying, 'It was just a dog; people are killed all the time. Why are you making such a big deal out of this police dog being killed?' And if that's their point of view, that's their point of view," Benny told me. "I look at our police dogs as members of this force. They may not be sworn members, but these are members. All these dogs care about is going out and looking for the bad guys, drugs and explosives."

Benny concluded, "These dogs are trained in a specific way, but when you get that opportunity to be so used to them and be with them so much, they become more than that. They become members of the unit and department, and a good deal of the officers feel that they are police officers just like anybody else."

The loss of a police dog and how it affects human officers can vary be department, Benny added. "We are a large department and have 34 dogs," he said. "I think a lot of times, smaller departments take it even worse then we would take it because there are only a few officers."

Officer Scott Johnson also had time to reflect on events. "It was nice to see so many people you never met in life to come to the service of a dog and for policemen that they didn't know," he said. "Some people just came up and said some remarkable things. A lady at the service gave me a St. Francis on a cross medallion, which was interesting because we are Catholic anyway, and I've carried it every day since then. I will never forget that."

Bo's death and the community's response helped show Scott that the work he puts in every day is really worth it and appreciated. "It's also nice to have a nice little plaque and the urn we keep Bo's ashes in," he said. "I also received a nice paw impression they took. A lot of things I wish I could have known about and done for my first dog. He didn't die in the line of duty, but he died while still in service. It's good that pet memorial services are bringing to light how much these dogs really sacrifice and do for the community."

Scott now has a new dog named Tex. "I got him two months or so after Bo died, and at first, it didn't seem quite right," he said. "We had two other mutt-type dogs that stay in the house that we had adopted, and they loved Bo to death and would play with him. He was their buddy and brother and everything else. When we'd found them, we'd just gotten Bo, and they would go and stand by the car every day after Bo died waiting for him. They'd also stand by his crate in the house." Even the family cat acted a little weird for awhile, he said.

But Scott's other dogs started feeling better when he brought Tex home, and so did his wife. "It took a little time at first, but it helped because it got me back to doing the job," he said. Scott also has a second police dog that works in the department's bomb unit. This dog, he keeps outside. "A lot of how you reward detection dogs is through a ball and praise, and she'd be a 70 pound lap dog if I let her in the house," he explained. "All she wants is attention."

These days, Bo continues spending time with the family on a shelf where the urn containing his cremated remains sits. "It's where we watch TV because he always watched TV with us," Scott explained. "The more I talk about it, I think the better it makes you feel just because you get to let it out instead of trying to bottle it all up. This is an important part of the process of letting go."

Lt. Benny Diggs Speaks About the History of Canines at his Department

The day-to-day work of these police dogs has always been intriguing to me, just like others. I had a chance to talk with Lt. Diggs about the history of the K-9 department. The following information comes directly from Lt. Benny Diggs, who explains the many meaningful contributions police dogs have made to the Indianapolis Police Department. While our department here in Indianapolis has its own intricacies, I'm sure our K-9 force looks like many across the United States. Below is some information straight from Lt. Diggs on the history of the department.

The Indianapolis Police Department first started its canine unit in 1960. It received initial training with the St. Louis, Mo., Police Department.

The Marion County Sheriff's implemented its canine unit in about 1965, and its officers were trained by the Indianapolis Police Department. Both the Indianapolis Police and Marion County Sheriff's Department started their individual canine units with two dogs each. As the years passed, it became evident how important a well trained canine unit can be when it comes to reducing crime. Each department added dogs to their respective teams.

In August 2006, a consolidation of the canine units at the two departments occurred. It was completed Jan. 1, 2007.

Since 1986, both departments combined have lost six dogs killed in the line of duty. One dog was killed by an automobile while attempting to apprehend a suspect who had escaped from jail in another jurisdiction. Five others were shot and killed. Three of those dogs lost their lives while saving their handlers or the lives of other officers.

The Indianapolis Metropolitan Police Department trains its dogs in criminal apprehension, tracking, area searches, narcotics and bomb detection.

The most important part of any canine unit is the dog selection process. A Police Service Dog (PSD) has to have a certain drive to do its job effectively. Regardless of how much the dog is trained – if the dog doesn't have specific drives that are needed to do a certain task – the dog will never be able to do that task at a level that is necessary to be an effective PSD.

Training improves the skill level of dogs' drives, and training provides confidence to complete a task. Proper training will take a particular drive or drives and teach the dog to effectively do a certain task. While training a PSD, we take a particular drive such as the ability to play, retrieve and search and turn those drives into the ability to be a detector dog. Regardless of what people may have heard in the past, we do not give our dogs any narcotic substance to enhance their ability to find narcotics. Nor do we give a dog substances that would enhance their ability to find explosives. This training is completely done by play, retrieving, repetition and motivation.

One thing that the public needs to recognize is that a PSD is a well trained tool in criminal apprehension. That PSD may deter criminal activity or the dog itself may apprehend a criminal or locate drugs, explosives or bodies.

The most important part of a PSD is its nose, which in my opinion is at least 90 percent of what makes a dog such a useful police tool. A dog's ability to apprehend a criminal is also very important. When I was on SWAT, I will never forget having a murder suspect who was hiding in a warehouse after killing an employee. A PSD who was assigned to a SWAT team officer was deployed, and within two minutes had located the suspect who had taken his own life.

Any police department's canine unit is only as good as its dog /handler team, training and an ability to use PSDs in daily situations.

Officer Scott Johnson receives condolences and an award for Bo from Sheriff Frank Anderson and Police Chief Michael Spears.

CHAPTER 12

Other Animal Heroes

Tom Flynn, president of Hillcrest Memorial Park and its People and Pet Gardens in Hermitage, Pa., with his service dog, Derek. The golden retriever is well known throughout the funeral profession and is a grief counselor for families.

Bo and the other police dogs like him aren't the only animal heroes.

As I've tried to share throughout this book, the cats, dogs and other beloved pets that are there with us on a daily basis are all heroes in their own right. They are always there for us, and they give back just as much – if not more – than we give.

I could fill an entire book about stories of dogs who notify their owners about a fire or a child in trouble. There are also so many stories about dogs saving someone from drowning or chasing away a burglar or someone else who would do their owners harm. Cats and other pets can also be quite courageous.

However, there are some animals that distinguish themselves like few others. Bo and the other police dogs like him obviously fall into this camp. But let's take a moment to remember, honor and pay tribute to just a few animals that have given back so much to the world. While some of these might not be an animal we typically think of as a "pet," I've come to realize throughout my career working with people that we can form close bonds with a variety of animals.

As a lifelong pet lover, I have found animals in history interesting. Come with me as I share some of the fabulous stories from our past. While this is by no means an exhaustive list, I do hope to drive home my point – we should appreciate these animals and not for a minute discount all their contributions, the unconditional love, and their unique personalities and spirits.

King Neptune the Pig

Most of this book has been dedicated to the cats and dogs in our lives, but King Neptune was a pig who died in 1950 in Mount Pleasant, Ill., and he deserves a place in this book.

As the unofficial mascot for the U.S. Navy for nine years, King Neptune helped raise more than $19 million in war bonds during World War II. That amount of money would be worth about $200 million today. Weighing 700 massive pounds, he was repeatedly auctioned off throughout the country to raise money in war bonds. Like we do with our pets today, he'd often be dressed up. Normally, you'd see him wearing a navy blue robe and gold crown. Those dressing him up would even paint his toenails.

As terrible as it sounds, King Neptune would have met an early demise if a Navy recruiter named Don C. Lingle hadn't struck upon the idea of auctioning the pig off instead of eating him. There must have been something special about the great pig, because everyone who bought him returned him to be auctioned again. Lingle and auctioneer L. Oard Sitter journeyed throughout southern Illinois auctioning off King Neptune. At one point, Illinois Gov. Dwight H. Green bought the pig for $1 million on March 6, 1943, on behalf of the people of his state.

At times, individual parts of King Neptune were auctioned off, such as his squeal or his bristles. It was all done to help the country with the war effort.

King Neptune did a great deal to help his country – even if he did so unknowingly. Nevertheless, there must have been something about his personality that helped him excel at this role. His sendoff, however, wasn't very elaborate, and for a long time his grave sat at a roadside rest stop. The gravestone reads, "Buried here – King Neptune, famous Navy mascot pig auctioned for $19,000,000.00 in war bonds 1942-1946 to help make a free world."

In June 2005, the powers that be had second thoughts about the modest grave, and the Illinois department of Transportation built a new memorial honoring King Neptune at the Trail of Tears Welcome Center on Interstate 57 North.

Simon the Cat:

Another pet whose heroics are well documented is Simon the Cat, who protected the food stored on the HMS Amethyst from rats. He managed to do this even after being injured when Chinese Communist forces shelled his British ship.

The shelling of the Amethyst is known as the Yangtze incident. When the ship returned to port, Simon was welcomed as a hero, and his shrapnel wounds were treated. He died about three weeks after being wounded, and he was buried with full military honors at the PDSA Animal Cemetery in Ilford, Essex. The People's Dispensary for Sick Animals is a veterinary charity that was founded in 1917 by Maria Dickin. It is the leading veterinary charity in the United Kingdom.

The cat's heroics are no joke. After his death, Simon was awarded the Dickin Medal for bravery – which the PDSA created in 1943. The award is considered the animal equivalent of the Victory Cross. Simon was even given the rank of "Able Seaman."

Cmdr. Stuart Hett told The Sun newspaper in a November 2007 report, "Simon's company and expertise as a rat-catcher were invaluable during the months we were held captive." He added, "During a terrifying time, he helped boost the morale of many young sailors, some of whom had seen their friends killed. Simon is still remembered with great affection."

Other Dickin Award Winners: The PDSA pet cemetery in England has honored other brave pets. There are dozens of other animals buried there who are considered heroes by their military handlers and owners.

There is Gander, a black Newfoundland dog who became the mascot of the Royal Rifles regiment and who became a sergeant. Gander died in 1941 when he grabbed a live grenade that would have exploded near several infantrymen during the Battle of Lye Mun on Hong Kong. He died because the grenade exploded in his mouth.

Beach Comber was a pigeon serving in the Canadian army when he brought the first news to England about an enemy landing.

Peter, a search and rescue dog, helped locate victims who were trapped under buildings that were bombed by the Germans. He served with the Ministry of Aircraft Production attached to the Civil Defense of London.

In all, 62 animals have received the Dickin Award. Not all of them, however, are buried at the cemetery. Some of their remains are buried closer to their handlers.

Everyday Heroes

A quick scan of the Internet will yield dozens of other animal heroes.

The "My Hero" project, which can be found at www.myhero.com, collects stories to celebrate the best of humanity – and this includes the special contributions that animals make in our lives. Here are a few of the animal heroes included on the site:

Binti Jua, an 8-year-old western lowland gorilla was at the Brookfield Zoo in Chicago, Ill., when she saw a 3-year-old child climb a railing and fall into her exhibit. She beat zoo officials to the boy and carried him to safety where personnel could easily tend to him. If she hadn't done so, it's unknown whether the other gorillas would have been so kind upon realizing an intruder was in their midst.

Balto gained fame as a sled dog. He's believed to have been a Siberian husky or Alaskan malamute, and he was named after Norwegian explorer Samuel Balto.

Balto led a team of sled dogs from 1922 to 1933, and he saved lives in Nome, Alaska, by helping to transport a serum to respond to a deadly diphtheria outbreak. The team of dogs he led had to travel more than 1,000 miles from Anchorage to Nome.

Ginny was a schnauzer and Siberian husky mix born in 1988 who lived on Long Beach Island. The dog became well known for rescuing kittens and cats. The dog always befriended cats in need, and she would cuddle up to them. She is credited with saving more than 900 cats, and she has a charity in her name, the Ginny Fund. Two books are written about her exploits. According to the

My Hero site, Ginny also once saved a blind man who stepped into traffic by barking to alert him of oncoming cars.

Sept. 11 Working Dogs

A number of dogs helped search for survivors after the Sept. 11 terrorist attacks, and all of these working dogs as well as those that serve every day in the military are definitely heroes. Sadly, there were very few – if any – survivors to be found after the attacks.

Jake, a black Labrador, is just one example of many. According to a July 26, 2007 article published by The Associated Press, Jake died from cancer. But during his career, he helped search for survivors in the debris of the terrorist attacks, and he also helped rescue people from the devastation of Hurricane Katrina.

Jake's owner, Mary Flood, is a member of Utah Task Force 1, which is a federal search-and-rescue team. She adopted Jake after finding him abandoned in the street with a broken leg. He was one of only a couple hundred U.S. government certified rescue dogs when he died, and he also helped train other dogs. "He was a great morale booster wherever he went," Flood told The Associated Press. "He was always ready to work, eager to play – and a master at helping himself to any unattended food items."

It's unknown if Jake and other rescue dogs like him developed cancer and other ailments as a result of the conditions under which they worked. The American Kennel Club Canine Health Foundation along with the Iams Company and The University of Pennsylvania sought to determine the effects of working in the rubble when they launched a five-year study of 17 dogs that helped in the recovery efforts.

Bomb-Sniffing Dogs Help Out in the War on Terror

The Sept. 11, 2001, terrorist attacks didn't just change our lives – it changed the lives of our animal companions, too.

A number of bomb-sniffing dogs have been specially trained to help the Marines serving in Afghanistan avoid improvised explosive devices. Marines trying to rebuild the nation and hunt down terrorists use metal detectors, ground penetrating radar and other equipment to detect explosives. But one of their chief assets is the specially-trained dogs that walk alongside them.

There were recently 12 dogs serving in Afghanistan, according to an August 2010 report by CBS News. These dogs have to contend with temperatures over 110 degrees, just like the soldiers. The only difference is that they are covered in fur.

The dogs that serve the Marines are equipped with a subcutaneous saline solution to keep them hydrated. Just like police officers, the bond between soldier handlers and the dogs they work with can become very close.

One of the dogs serving in Afghanistan, Tar, died in an explosion when he started sniffing and set off an IED by pressing down on it. His handler, Jonathan Melbourne, lost his right eye and broke his right arm, but he's expected to recover from his injuries. When Tar set off the bomb, he was in front of a platoon of about 30 people. Melbourne has said publicly if Tar didn't set off the explosion, someone in the unit surely would have stepped on the device and been killed.

As noted, I could write an entire book about the tremendous things that pets and animals have done to help their animal companions. Let us all remember our own hero pets, too, who greet us every morning when we wake up and when we come home from work. They are without-a-doubt true heroes to every pet parent who loves them. With that, they deserve to be treated well in life and honored with respect and dignity in death.

Dear Pet Heroes

While I sit here in awe of everything that you do for us, all I can humbly say to you is "Thank You." Whether you are a K-9 police officer, a search-and-rescue dog, a cat who provides emotional support, or a gorilla who has assisted a fellow human being, "thank you" seems so small for what you selflessly give to us, mankind.

I am humbled by the unconditional love that you share with us. In good times and bad, you give love. You fully trust that we, your human caretakers, will give you what you need. For all of these qualities, I can only aspire to be as loving, trusting and caring as you are to us. Yes, I do believe that those qualities of an animal are why we love you so much – you are made up of those attributes that represent something special.

So, again, I thank you for all that you do for us. For those heroes that the world knows about to those silent heroes that reside in the comfort and care of each of our homes. Thank you for blessing us with your spirit and your unconditional love.

For that, we are eternally grateful.

Love,
Coleen

CHAPTER 13

Planning Ahead for that Terrible Moment

A family plans ahead for their beloved Maggie with a pre-planned headstone at the Hinsdale Animal Cemetery and Crematory in Illinois.

Preparing yourself in advance for the death of your pet, while emotionally taxing, is a wise and thoughtful thing to do. Certainly none of us likes to think of that day, the day our heart will be broken into a million pieces. Thinking about this ahead of time will give you and your family the opportunity to discuss how you would like to memorialize your beloved pet and to celebrate the life that you all shared together.

There are numerous elements to think about regarding the death of your pet and your final wishes. Take this time to reflect upon what your pet will need in respectful death-care treatment, as well as the support you will need as a grieving pet parent. Making sure that our beloved pets are treated with the dignity and respect that they deserve will be of the utmost importance at this time. Knowing your various options will relieve much of the stress you may have in ensuring what you do is appropriate to not only honor the life of your pet but to ensure that they are receiving the care and treatment in death that they deserve.

The questions and information included in this chapter will help you determine how to handle the death of a beloved pet.

Final Arrangements

The final arrangement wishes for my pet's body is:

_____Burial _____Cremation

Influences to help shape your decision for burial or cremation are:

If burial, where?

_____ Home _____Friend's Home

_____Local Pet Cemetery

Areas of consideration with this decision are:
- Will this town/county/development allow pet burials?
- Will you always live in this area or have access to this burial ground?
- Do your religious preferences guide you in one way or another?
- Did your pet like the outside or the inside? Will that influence your pet's final resting place?

For burial, will you want a casket to protect the pet's body?

_____Yes _____No

If cremation, will you want the ashes returned?

_____Yes _____No

If this answer is **no**, you need to ask your pet death-care provider for a "group" cremation or "communal" cremation. Your pet will be cremated with other pets, their ashes scattered in a designated area.

For cremation, is it important to you to have your pet's body cremated **alone** in the crematory?

_____ Yes _____No

If this answer is **yes**, many death care providers will have the option of a "private" cremation. Your pet's body will be solo in the crematory, ensuring that the returned ashes are only your pet.

Many death-care providers will provide a tracking system through the cremation process, a "tag" with a unique number that will accompany the pet's body. To ensure the safety, security and authentication of the cremation process, inquiring about this part of your pet death-care provider's policy will give you the peace of mind in knowing about the care of your pet's mortal remains.

Service Options

Many families will also want to have that one last time to visit their pet after death, a visitation or wake, if you will. While this may seem like a trivial thing – or possibly something that you consider morbid and odd, this one last time with your pet is valuable time spent. It is a time to see your pet at peace, a time for your children to pay tribute by bringing in items that were special to your pet and a time to begin the grief journey and to say that final goodbye. Remember what Steve Cardwell said about this time – "it's the one event that I am most thankful for – and one that I did not know that I needed!"

Many times, other friends, family members and other pets in the household will want to have their final goodbye with your pet, too. Pets touch so many people during their short lives with us. Allow those around you the opportunity to come together, pay their respects, and support each other.

My family and I will want a final goodbye time with our pet:

_____Yes _____No

Occasionally families will take this final goodbye time to incorporate their important family/religious rituals. Rituals may look like:

- Special readings
- Rituals you and your pet did to say, "I love you"
- A candle lighting tribute
- Reading of special poems and remembrances
- Scripture readings
- A special planting of a tree/flower/bush
- A donation drive for a local shelter in memory of your pet

The following rituals are important and will be included in our final goodbye time together:

_____

_____

_____

_____

_____

_____

_____

Memorialization Options

Making a decision on memorialization products is a personal process. This will be reflective of the life shared with your pet, your lifestyle, your personal style, and those items that are reflective of your pet's personality.

There are various memorialization products:

- Rocks/garden flagstones
- An urn that is reflective of your decorating style
- An urn with paw prints to show your love of animals
- A personalized urn made to look like the pet
- Locket jewelry to hold a bit of the pet's ashes or hair
- Jewelry that would have the pet's own paw print or nose print on it
- An eco-friendly urn for burial in a special location
- A piece of art done to depict your pet's personality
- A frame to hold a cast of your pet's paw print, nose print, and locket of hair
- Memorial note cards

A guide in purchasing an urn:

- What is the personality of my pet – will I want an urn that depicts that? For example, would you say:
    - "She was a 'girly-girl' requiring something feminine-looking?"
    - "My boy was all boy – the need is for something strong and bold!"
- Where will the urn go in your home?
    - Should the urn blend in or to stand out?
    - Considering the décor of the area where the urn will be—what are the other items surrounding the urn?
- Are there other pets at home?

- Consider a larger "family" urn for all pets to be together.
- Will the urn eventually be buried – or will the urn be buried with you or another family member as part of their final arrangements?

As families decide on the personalization of memorial products, it can be overwhelming to sum up and reflect on a pet's life in a few words. This personalization may be something that you are considering for an urn, a rock or marker for the burial spot or for a special spot outside, a death notice card, or various other pieces that you will want to truly capture who your pet was, their personality, or what you will think of when you say their name. Furthermore, hearing other friends and family members' stories is certainly a wonderful way to reflectively pay tribute to your pet and get everyone involved in honoring their life. Consider:

When you think about your pet – what makes you smile?

- A nickname
  - "He was our little Buddy-Wuddy"
  - "Whit"
  - "Squirrelly-Girly-Shirley"
  - "Lover Boy"
  - "Sweetie Pie"
- A saying
  - "Hiding sox in heaven"
  - "Always Chasing Frisbees and Hearts"
  - "Our First Born"
  - "She's My Girl, Daddy"
- Dates
  - Birth date to death date
  - Gotcha date to death date
- A photo
- Personal paw print or nose print
- A bone
- A heart
- Their favorite treat—a slice of pizza
- Another favorite treat—a cookie
- A favorite activity – a ball, a Frisbee, a certain type of toy, a Kong

A Tribute to My Pet's Life

Pet's Name_____

Birth date/Gotcha date — Death date_____

Nicknames_____

Where born/Where Gotcha'd_____

You came to live at our house when we found you here: _____

Pet Parents_____

Siblings – Pet and Human_____

Favorite Toy(s)_____

Favorite Activity(s)_____

Least Favorite Thing_____

Other friends _____

Favorite Place to Sleep_____

Favorite Food _____

What I will remember most about our life together:

_____

What I learned from you in the life we shared together was:

_____

What you represented in our house was: _____

Your personality was:

_____

Children and Pet Loss

For many children, the loss of a pet might be their first experience with death. And, subsequently, this will be the first experience for parents in guiding their child through the emotions, rituals, and ultimately their grief journey as they remember this furry love that they had in their lives.

Children grieve in a way that is very natural. For parents, it's important to allow this grief and mourning to happen and to be there to support your child. You also should have some humility and realize that children will want to do this process in their way, a way that might be considered unusual, out of the ordinary, or uncomfortable for the adults in the house. However, it's important to let the child express their emotions fully and to honor the time that they shared with their pet in the way that they want to.

The grief journey and the mourning process will vary with children according to their age. However, regardless of the age, there are certain things that will always be true:

- They will need to say goodbye – to see the deceased body of their special pet and know that it's okay to pet the body and to kiss their special pet on the head.
- They will use the adults in their life as a barometer as to how they think they should act. As adults, it's important that we let the child know that we are hurting too and that it's okay to show your emotions through crying.

For many children, I encourage them to write the pet a letter – or to write a letter about their pet. For the younger children, it may also be drawing a picture of the pet or for the pet. For some children, as an adult you may need to guide them with a template for the letter.

If the child is old enough to understand journaling, then I fully recommend this as well.

Creating a Tribute Table

Another wonderful activity to do with children is the creation of a Tribute Table. This table is a visual reminder to the child of all things that were important to that pet or about that pet in the life they shared with your family. Setting up a Tribute Table is easy and one that every member of the family will truly find healing as they honor a life that was shared:

1. Dedicate a table in the house for the Tribute Table. This might be a sofa table, an end table, or a card table.
2. As a family, remember all of those things that were important to the pet. This might look like:

a. Their treats

b. Their toys

c. Their blanket

d. Their collar and leash

e. Their pillow

f. Their favorite shirt

g. A favorite CD of music

h. Their food bowl

3. As a family, remember all of those things that were important about the pet. This might look like:

a. Family photos

b. Their birth certificate/adoption certificate

c. Awards from contests they were in

d. Their urn

e. A fur clipping

f. Letters from the family

g. Cards received when the pet died

h. Flowers

i. A candle

4. Throughout the time frame set, a week, for instance, when anyone in the family remembers something special about the pet, it should be added to the table.

5. At the end of the time period specified, set a time to gather as a family. This time could be used to:

a. Tell stories about the pet

b. Light a candle in memory of the pet

c. Tell others what was learned from the pet

d. What will be missed most about the pet

e. Favorite nicknames

f. Special readings

g. Playing special music

A Tribute Table that shows everything important in a life that was shared together.

Children want the opportunity to pay tribute to their special pet friend, too. Give them this by letting them share special photos, letters, notes, and other items of significance at a ceremony. The worksheet that follows can also be used to help children express their feelings.

remembering my pet...

Write a letter to your pet, thanking him or her for the
many memories you made together....

Dear _____

_____

_____

_____

_____

_____

_____

_____

Draw a picture of you and your pet...

CHAPTER 14

The Intricacies of Pet Loss

When you mention the word "death" to almost anyone, he or she will either change the topic or say outright, "I don't want to talk about it."

However, even though people avoid the topic, most people empathize with losing a loved one. When I mentioned to anyone that my dad died, so many people told me "my sympathies" or "I'm sorry." The feedback made me feel better, and it showed that people cared.

The situation is different when a pet parent suffers a loss. While 62 percent of our society owns a pet, this means 38 percent of the population does not. Therefore, should I, a grieving pet parent, happen to mention the fact that my pet died to one of those 38 percent, the responses that I get might not be so caring.

Some families I've worked with have been devastated by the responses they hear from others. For instance, we sometimes hear, "Your cat died? Those are a dime a dozen, why don't you just get another one?" to "Are you kidding me – you are crying over the death of a dog!" One of the more infuriating responses came from my stepdaughter's boss, who told her, "You know I hate animals. Why would I let you off work early for the death of yours?"

These types of responses do not convey any empathy or respect, and it makes it hard for the pet owner to show his or her emotions and deal with the loss.

For so many grieving pet parents, when a pet dies, we feel grief and an internal loss. However, many times we won't allow ourselves to mourn, to physically show our grief, because we feel silly or we feel like those around us will think that we are silly if we show these emotions. Therefore, we will grieve, but we won't mourn.

My mentor, Dr. Alan Wolfelt, likes to say, "He who has no time to mourn has no time to mend." This is an important point, and we need to mourn these losses in order to begin our grief journeys.

The loss of a pet brings with it what I call "The Intricacies of Pet Loss." These are the issues that come with the loss of a pet but generally not with the loss of a human loved one. Following are some nuances that a pet parent may need to navigate during a grief journey.

The Deafening Silence

When Mico died, she was my only pet at home. The first time I went home after she died, the silence in the house was so incredibly loud it scared me. The silence began to scream at me, to yell at me, to constantly shout at me that my pretty girl was no longer there.

After a while, the deafening silence made me feel like I was losing my mind. Whenever I stepped back into my home, it served as a cold, stark reminder of the situation. As loud as it was, the silence played tricks with my head. At times, I thought I heard her bark or her nails on the hardwood floor, coming down the hallway. I also thought I felt her weight at night, lying next to me on the bed in her favorite spot. To think that she was still there and then wake up and realize that she was truly gone was an incredibly hurtful and empty feeling.

These types of things took me fully by surprise. Months later, as I stood back and began to process everything, I realized that others felt it, too. It didn't matter if there was one pet at home or many pets; the deafening silence had an impact on anyone who had a close bond with a pet that died.

To the relief of families, I began to bring this up with them when I was companioning them through their loss. Others felt the same way as I did, but they just didn't know how to put it into words. I could recognize someone who was going through the same thing that I went through because they would start their sentences with something like, "I feel like I'm losing my mind . . ."

This deafening silence can be tough to take. The stark reality of the presence of the absence can make just getting through the day a chore.

The Special Bond

As I have already mentioned, 62 percent of people in the United States own pets. The remaining 38 percent usually do not know what it means to have a special bond with a pet.

For so many grieving hearts, the loss of a pet brings about the desire to have our loss and our feelings validated. It's important that the grief we feel be respected. Just as when a human dies, it's essential to have a support system that activates when we need it most. Sometimes, we just want someone to talk to, and of course, we want to honor the story of our beloved pets by sharing our memories of them with others.

It hurts my heart when I hear the raw emotions of grief from a family who has just lost a precious pet. But my heart hurts even more when I hear from someone who isn't getting the support they need from the "friends" around them. Sometimes, these "friends" can actually make the situation much worse by criticizing the grief that someone feels. Worse yet is when well-meaning friends shame a pet parent when they are actively mourning. They sometimes question someone who is crying over their deceased pet by saying "Why are you still crying over him? It's been a week."

Someday, these people may understand what it means to love a pet, but when you are trying to recover from a loss, it might be best to avoid them. It's important to understand who you can share your grief with and who will be there to truly support you in your grief journey. The first step in doing that is to know who really understands the relationship that you had with your pet when your pet was alive. Those are the people that you will want to turn to for support when your pet dies.

For us pet lovers, it truly is difficult to understand those people that have chosen, for whatever reason, to not have a pet in their life. However, we also need to know that they don't understand us either. It's not a question of who's right and who's wrong but more so a matter of respect for each other's differences.

Therefore, if there is a person in your life that is part of your support system and this person doesn't understand or respect the relationship you have with your pet, it will be difficult to turn to this person when the pet dies. Look for those pet lovers or those who unconditionally love you, respect you, and want to help you through difficult times. These are the people who will let you make your way through the grief journey in the way that's right for you.

Grief Ranking

For women in particular, our nature is to say that there are others who are worse off than we are. We justify our feelings in this manner and turn to our caregiver side to say "we shouldn't be hurting as there are others with larger issues."

Therefore, many times with the loss of our pet, we will find someone else in our life that's got it worse. We'll justify why we shouldn't be mourning our loss with excuses such as "Joe's mother died – and that must be a worse situation than ours" or "Betty's battling cancer – her issues are bigger than mine."

There's another way to look at this "grief ranking," which is a subject I lecture on when I guest teach at a local vet tech college. As I began speaking about this, one of the young ladies in the class began to sob uncontrollably. When she finally calmed down enough to speak, she said, "For all of these years I have been plagued with guilt because I always felt a bigger loss when my cat died than when my brother died. I always thought I was a horrible person for that."

It broke my heart to see this young lady, who's obviously been torn about this for years, struggle with the guilt and the thought of being a bad person because of how she handled her cat's death compared with her brother's death.

For some, it may seem odd, but we should feel the loss for what it is and what it meant in our life. Our animals bring to us unconditional love and acceptance. It's natural to feel different emotions when they die than what we feel for our human loved ones. None of these deaths should be ranked to mean more than another. They should all be felt in the way that's right for us and for our heart.

Questions of Faith

If I've heard the question once I've heard it a thousand times – "Do pets go to heaven?" With the exception of a few families that I've dealt with, this question burns in everyone's mind.

This intricacy of pet loss is an incredibly interesting topic. I find it interesting that when we lose a human loved one, spiritual people focus on how good the person was and think that it's natural for the person to reign in heaven, the ultimate home.

However, when a pet dies, so many people have an opinion on this topic, to the point of literally hurting a bereaved heart. It's amazing to me what people relay to me that they've had others say to them on the question of whether pets go to heaven.

Here are some examples of what some people say:

"There's no way—pets don't have souls."

"There's no way – the Bible does not reference this. Therefore, it's not true."

"Nope. Nope. Nope. I will not go to a heaven where these creatures are."

There are many arguments like the ones above, and while I don't want to make this book a vehicle to promote religious beliefs, I also believe it helps a grieving heart to believe in the mystery. A person's faith allows them to believe in what it is they want to believe in. Therefore, if I openly say that I believe pets go to heaven, my feelings should be respected. Likewise, other grieving pet parents who feel the same way should have their feelings respected, too.

The point is: I respect those that don't believe animals go to heaven. I've made a conscious effort to avoid debating this topic. I'd ask everyone to let us believe in what we want to believe! There is no reason to argue about such a personal belief.

As I've told many grieving hearts who wonder about pets and heaven, "Opinions are like bellybuttons, or whatever other body part you want to use – we've all got one." My opinion is that I want to keep the faith and believe what I believe. However, at a time of loss and grief, the last thing that needs to happen is to debate religion and beliefs.

I just want to believe in the mystery. Because, really, when it's all over, how will you really know if I was right or if I was wrong?

CHAPTER 15

Living the Loss

Mike the Dog in a Halloween costume.

Throughout the process of writing this book, I've been moved and honored to pay tribute to the wonderful pet children that have affected so many lives. It was an emotional experience reliving all of this.

It became even more emotional, however, when I looked up one day and realized that I would be facing the loss of another one of my own precious pets. My 15-year-old golden retriever, Mike the Dog had become frail and weak.

I was struck by just *how* old he'd become one night while sitting out on the veranda sipping a cup of hot tea and enjoying a few minutes of play with Mike the Dog before bedtime. This time, he was a bit slower than normal, and I noticed how gray he'd become. Even though he was 15, I'd never seen him as old. He still played with the other dogs and acted much younger than his old-man age. Denial can be a wonderful place to hide and exist. Deep down, I had noticed how much he'd slowed down, but it was a lot easier emotionally to overlook it.

But a new reality was setting in. Mikey was slowing down, his breathing was becoming more labored, and he no longer could walk up and down stairs. I made an internal commitment that I would become even more aware of him and his needs, physically and emotionally, knowing full well that my time with him was becoming limited. I wasn't sure how much more aware I could be with him – as I pride myself in knowing my pets and what they need or what they are saying. I wanted to make the remaining time I had with him as joyful and comfortable as I could.

With the realization that the beginning of the end was staring me in the face, I began to make strategic plans for the inevitable. I gently relayed my observations to Chris, who had brought Mike the Dog into our family when we were married. Mikey had been accepted into our family with open arms, and Chris would not accept my observation. I could sympathize, because I had not wanted to accept what was happening to our sweet and precious dog myself.

We soon began to discuss with Amy and Brian these final days. We did not use the "E" word because that would make the situation too real, too fast. Instead, we were all hoping that one day or one night, Mike the Dog would make the decision for us and just die peacefully in his sleep. This request was in my nightly prayers.

Hard Times

But the days progressively became worse. His breathing became even more labored and his body even weaker. It was not the beginning of the end that was staring me in the face; we were clearly in the final days of his journey here on earth.

The summer heat became more intense, and this did not help Mike in his already-labored breathing. My heart ached for him as he went outside for his normal doggie duties and then struggled to get himself back to the cool of the house. Being a proud Golden Retriever, he did what he could to help himself before asking for support up the stairs. However, I could tell that it really pained him to have to be helped. He was such a proud boy and would rather have done it all himself.

However, even here at the end of his earthly existence, Mike the Dog still went outside to do what he loved most – The Golden Roll! He would slowly inch his way to the ground and then roll over on his back and then give it his all to roll around! He got such pleasure from doing this that I do believe I could almost hear him laughing as he did it. I knew that the first snowfall without him would be tough because we always loved to see the angels that he would make in the freshly fallen snow.

With this newfound realization that Mike was old, I scrambled to make sure that we captured every bit of our last days together as a family. I suddenly realized that I did not have a good portrait of him so I quickly hired a photographer to come to our home to capture the entire family together. Yes, the heat bothered him for the photo shoot, but the fact that there were people at our home to pay attention to him was more important. He looked so handsome in the photos! I will forever treasure these last photos of him and our family.

The entire Ellis-Burke family enjoys some time together.

The Prognosis

The Fourth of July weekend was upon us. Chris had come home to attend a vet appointment that I had scheduled for Mike. I wanted him to hear from Dr. Day what the prognosis was and what we should do next.

The veterinarian ran a blood panel on Mikey and covered all of her bases. She found a slight infection based on an elevated white blood cell count, but there was nothing else significantly wrong with him. Except of course for the obvious – he was old, and she could tell he was tired and shutting down.

As we talked about our next steps, we considered increasing Mike's heart medication to relieve the fluid buildup on his lungs. We talked about an antibiotic for his infection. I talked about all of these things, knowing full well that I was really avoiding the word that neither one of us wanted to hear.

But then Dr. Day said it: the "E" word: "euthanasia."

I looked at Chris and both of us immediately had tears in our eyes.

A Hard Decision

We drove home in silence, and I took my anger out on Dr. Day. "Why on earth would she say the 'E' word when I know that we have other avenues to pursue to make him better?" I asked Chris.

He didn't answer. He knew the answer.

The weekend was busy with holiday activities. However, not far from our minds and our thoughts were Mikey and what needed to happen. Everyone in the house was feeling emotional. Even our other pets – Crisco, Rudy and Ellie – who are normally well behaved, acted out on more than one occasion. After numerous episodes of unacceptable pet behavior, Chris asked, "Do you think that the animals are trying to tell us something?" I didn't answer, but I knew that he was right. The animals always know.

While Mike did get a bit worse over the weekend, I remained in denial. I held close in my heart that something positive was going to happen and that he would be back to his old self again. I continued to hold on to the belief that everyone else, including our other animals, were wrong. Mike was going to be OK.

The kids came over for dinner and spent time with Mike. While he didn't move around much anymore, his loud golden bark was constantly a stark reminder that he was indeed here and in the house! He loved Brian and Amy, always perking up when they arrived and remembering his human brother and sister with such gusto!

The holiday weekend spilled over to Tuesday that week. On Monday, Chris and I had the inevitable conversation. It was decided that the following Friday would be the day. Chris would drive home early from work, we would have Dr. Day come to the house, and our entire family would be there for Mikey. With the decision being made, the air in the house became even heavier. Now, we were not on a deathwatch but a death march. Marching toward Friday and "E" day.

Trudging Toward a Terrible Moment

Chris woke up early for his drive back to Chicago on Tuesday morning. The air in the bedroom, where, of course everyone slept, two-legged and four-legged – was heavier than normal. Chris took his time in saying goodbye to all of the pets, with extra time being spent in talking to Mikey. As he leaned down to talk to Mikey, who slept on the floor on my side of the bed, Rudy made his way over to the edge of the bed near Chris's bent over body and put his paw on Chris's arm, as if to say, "Please don't go. We are going to need you here today."

I got up not long after Chris left to start my day. As with any household with numerous pets, feeding time is always an adventure. Getting bowls filled, keeping the cat out of the dog bowls and the dogs out of the cat bowl, medicines and vitamins dispensed, water bowls filled. In essence – never a dull moment.

Generally, the minute Mike would hear food bowls rattling, he'd treat it like an alarm clock and come to the kitchen. On this particular morning, that didn't happen. I went into the bedroom and had to wake him up and then help him to stand. Making his way down the hallway, he fell three times. I knew that it was going to be a trying day for all of us.

The day progressed, and Mike got worse right in front of me. He did not want his dog food so I made him a turkey sandwich with peanut butter. He could barely eat it, lying down on the floor and turning his head to the side to consume the food. This was the first time that I had ever seen him not take great pleasure in eating.

But the clearest and loudest sign came from Rudy, my beautiful sensitive one-eared cat. On this day, he had made it his duty to not leave Mike's side. He lay with him, he lay beside him, and he laid on him. I knew with that animal-to-animal action, my time with Mike was nearing the end. Rudy was doing what animals do to protect and pay their respects to the dying. He was showing his love and support with this physical act of love.

Saying Goodbye

As evening approached, I kept myself busy around the house before stepping outside to water the plants and flowers. When I came back inside – it was about 9:15 p.m. – I looked down and saw Mike lying on the floor. I noticed that he had urinated on the carpet very near where he was lying. As I looked closer at him, I saw that his tongue was sticking out the front of his mouth. I bent down near him and saw that his tongue was very dark. This was a clear indication that he was lacking oxygen.

I grabbed the phone and called Chris. "Mikey's dying right before my eyes," I started to cry.

Chris has always been the calm one, and this time was no different. However, my heart was aching for him, too. Here I was, with the dog that he brought home for the kids almost 15 years ago, and now this creature was dying. Being 3 hours away, I knew that Chris felt helpless.

"What do you think you should do?" he calmly asked me.

I looked down at Mike, now very clearly in the middle of leaving his earthly existence, and it hit me cold. "I'm going to hang up, hold him in my arms and let him die peacefully."

So, I did. I sat down on the floor and held his head in my hands and stroked his body, talking to him the entire time. Reminding him how much we loved him. Telling him to go, be at peace, to let this old body be new again. I wanted him to run in the heavens like he loved to do.

I continued talking to him, reminding him how much we loved him. I stayed close to his face so that he could smell that I was with him. At this time, a time when I would want my loved ones close to me, I wanted him to know that I was there.

A moment of sanity took over, and I dialed Dr. Day's number. I needed to have her here with me to tend to the medical side of Mike, even though I knew the outcome was going to be what it was.

I continued holding my precious dog, and finally, the last breath came. I looked at him and knew that my big boy was gone. I could almost feel his soul leave.

Mourning Our Loss

I sat there for a minute, still stroking Mike's head and holding him in my arms. The tears came harder. I picked up the phone and called Chris to let him know. Then I made the dreadful calls to Brian and Amy. Crying harder and harder each time I said the words, "Mikey died."

I took a few deep breaths and then began to really look at what had just happened. Here was my beautiful boy, in front of me – dead. I looked again. I realized that he looked peaceful and comfortable. It then dawned on me – I hadn't seen him this peaceful and comfortable in a very, very long time.

I took another look. I've seen thousands and thousands of deceased animals, but Mike the Dog had just died one of the prettiest deaths that I had seen. Amy would later comment that she felt like his "golden" came back.

Soon, people began arriving. Dr. Day was first, and next was Grandma Sharlene, who helped take care of our pets while we were away. Dr. Day told me the obvious, and Grandma Sharlene cried for this big love that she took care of often.

Then, Amy and her mom came over to say their goodbyes. All of us sat on the floor with our precious Mike, telling him how much we loved him, what a good boy he was and how much he would be missed.

Life without Mike the Dog Begins

I kept Mike's body with me overnight, right on the kitchen floor where he was comfortable. He was lying on a towel because I didn't want to cover him up. He always hated being covered with a blanket when he was alive, so I was quite sure that he would have hated it now as well.

This process also gave all of the other pets their time to say goodbye. Animals are organic mourners, and they mourn naturally. Crisco hung his head and looked like he had a tear in his eye. Ellie, I believe, had known a very long time ago that Mikey was dying, and she had said her goodbyes already. Rudy still elected to stay near Mike's body and perform his mourning rituals. It was important to me that they all had ample time to pay their respects to Mike, to do it in their own time and in their own way.

It really was a comfort for me to know that I still had Mike with me. Our dog loved to be with people, and the thought of him being taken away by the pet funeral home in the middle of the night and lying in a dark and empty building by himself was more than I could bear. It gave me an incredible sense of peace knowing that he was with his pet siblings and me.

As I woke up in the morning, I thought I heard Mike's nails clicking on the hallway floor. "What is he already doing up for breakfast? No one else is up yet," I said to myself. For a brief moment, I thought the events of the previous day were just a bad dream.

Then it hit me, like a ton of bricks. The nightmare was real. I got up as quickly as I could and made my way to the kitchen. There he was, just like I had left him last night. He still looked beautiful and peaceful, and the tears started again.

Trying to Move On

Pet Angel was going to be there by mid-morning, so I knew that I had some time I could spend with Mike. I also wanted to let Chris say goodbye to his big boy.

I connected with Chris on Skype and positioned the camera on Mike's body. For the next 30 minutes, we had our own techno-memorial service. We told stories, starting with the day that Chris found Mike at a breeder hiding behind a water heater. We worked our way up to the present moment, shedding lots of tears as we told our beautiful memories.

Brian showed up to get Mike. I felt horrible for him, and he told me, "I help other people with their pets. I don't want to do my own." I knew how hard it was for him – here he was picking up a dog that had come into his life when he was just a kid. As a young professional, a very large part of his life was coming to a close.

Brian found a pen and had me authorize the cremation before moving on to other meaningless paperwork. We all process these events in our own unique way, and this was the way that worked best for him.

In the typical Pet Angel way, Mikey was placed on a blanket and into a casket. Just knowing that his body would be treated respectfully because of this service that I started was so comforting. I helped Brian take him to the truck. Of course, I needed to give Mikey numerous kisses on the head and I let him know how much I loved him. It was hard to face the stark reality: I would never again see my golden boy's beautiful body again. That within itself took my mind reeling back through time, through all of the events over the years that he had been a part of. We would have to move into a new normal without this amazing love.

I was quite sure that there were no more tears in my body, but I found out that there were. I cried and cried and cried for the rest of the day. I just couldn't get comfortable. When I sat down, I felt like I needed to stand up. When I stood up I felt like I needed to lie down. When I lay down, I felt like I would be sick. And when I ate, it dawned on me that I wasn't hungry.

The entire day went by like this, and I just could not get comfortable. Everything around me reminded me of Mikey. Even though the other animals were still in the house, the house felt deathly quiet. The silence was deafening, and the clear presence of the absence was overwhelming.

Paying Tribute

I started creating Mike's Tribute Table. The flowers started coming in as well as the cards. I gathered up his food bowl and filled it with treats to put on the table. He loved treats! I draped his collar over the bowl – that always represented a walk, another event that he just loved. I played the music that always helped him relax. The whole table was about Mikey and his life.

A few days later, Mike's cremated remains were ready to be picked up. Amy wanted to be with me when I went so that she could pick out her special memorialization pieces as well. A frame with Mike's paw print and fur clipping, his special portrait, and a paw print charm necklace were all on her list. She loved her goofy golden and wanted to always remember him.

Everyone's grief journey continued, and we all walked the path in our own way. Chris was emotional at times, but he continued to say how thankful and grateful he was that Mike died the way that he did – on his own, at home and with me. Mike did it the way that he wanted to – and in the end, yes, it was very peaceful.

Amy, a bit reserved like her dad, remembered Mikey from the day her dad brought him home and throughout the wonderful life that they shared together as a family. Brian, even more reserved, moved on quickly and in his own way, too.

But for me, the tears were never very far from the surface. Every day was filled with "firsts" – or possibly "lasts," I never thought that doing poop pickup duty in the back yard would be a tearful experience, but that last one was! And, the first time that he was not included in the pickup process was another emotional day. There also was the first day of not filling his bowl, the first time when I walked in the door and realized that golden bark was missing and the first time I went out with the other animals without him. Moving forward, I know there are going to be more "firsts." They strike at odd times and sometimes when I least expect it.

While the pain at times seems unbearable, I also know that the only way that I could have avoided this grief journey, this pain, is to not have had this love in my life in the first place. That would be much too big a tradeoff. For you see, love and grief are equal. The unconditional love, the memories, and the joy that this big, beautiful creature brought to my family and me are worthy of every one of the tears that I have shed. I would not trade that for anything.

I think back to the special note that I sent with Mike on his final journey to the pet funeral home. The note summed up my thoughts about Mike and the life we shared together:

"I love you, My Big Boy, and I always will. I already miss you and will think of you daily.

Say 'hello' to Mico. Tell her I love her, I miss her, and every day I do what I do for her and you.

Rest in peace, Mike the Dog. Rest in peace."

Rest in peace, my precious babies. Rest in peace.

CHAPTER 16

Pet Loss Resources

For many pet parents, trying to find the appropriate resources for guidance on the death of a pet is difficult—whether it be the right pet loss organization to assist with the loss of a pet or resources to help you honor the memory of your pet.

You took an important step in buying this book, but I urge you to also seek out more information. There are numerous websites out there with information, including my own at www.TwoHeartsPetLoss.com. Some of the things you will find on the site are:

- Wonderful reading material
- Videos with information on dealing with the loss of a pet
- Coloring sheets to download for children
- A beautiful rendition of Rainbow Bridge
- An opportunity to post a photo of your precious pet and share your memories
- And much more

As I continually search the Internet for additional helpful sites, my heart is always warmed by the work that others are doing to support pet parents in the loss of their beloved pets. Although not an exhaustive list, here are a few other sites that I think are helpful for grieving pet parents:

www.HealFromPetLoss.com

www.Pet-Loss.net

www.PetRib.com

www.PetLoss.com

Reading Resources

If you are looking for other helpful books, following is a list that was shared with me from my friends at the Argus Institute at Colorado State University:

- "Goodbye My Friend" by Herb and Mary Montgomery
- "Journey Through Pet Loss" by D. Antinori
- "Grieving the Death of a Pet" by Betty J. Carmack
- "When Your Pet Dies: A Guide To Mourning, Remembering and Healing" by Dr. Alan D. Wolfelt, Ph.D.
- "Goodbye, Friend: Healing Wisdom for Anyone Who Has Ever Lost a Pet" by Gary Kowalski
- "Preparing for Pet Loss—A Final Act of Caring" by Herb and Mary Montgomery
- "Pets Living with Cancer: A Pet Owner's Resource" by R. Downing, DVM
- "Surviving the Heartbreak of Choosing Death for Your Pet: Your Personal Guide for Every Living Thing" by Cynthia Rylant
- "Old Dogs Remembered" by Bud Johns (ed.)
- "Angel By My Side" by Mike Lingenfelter
- "Angel Whiskers: Reflections on Loving and Losing a Feline Companion" by Laurel Hunt (ed.)
- "Dealing with Pet Euthanasia" by Linda Mary Peterson
- "Good Grief: Finding Peace After Pet Loss" by Sid Korpi

Helping Children with Pet Loss

- "Dog Heaven" by Cynthia Rylant
- "Cat Heaven" by Cynthia Rylant
- "For Every Dog an Angel" by Christine Davis
- "For Every Cat an Angel" by Christine Davis
- "A Special Place for Charlee: A Child's Companion Through Pet Loss" by Debra Morehead
- "A Gift From Rex" by Jim Kramer, DVM
- "The Tenth Good Thing About Barney" by Judith Viorst
- "Remembering My Pet" by N. Liss-Levinson, PhD and Rev. M. Phinney Baskette, MDiv
- "Talking About Death: A Dialogue Between Parent and Child" by Earl Grollman
- "When Your Pet Dies: Dealing With Your Grief and Helping Your Children Cope" by Christine Adamec
- "When Children Grieve" by John W. James

- "Healing the Bereaved Child" by Alan Wolfelt, Ph.D.
- "A Child's View of Grief" by Alan Wolfelt, Ph.D.
- "Healing Your Grieving Heart for Kids" by Alan Wolfelt, Ph.D.

Religious/Spiritual

- "Souls of Animals" by Gary Kowalski
- "Dogs Have Souls Too" by George and Emily Watson
- "Spirit Dogs: Heroes in Heaven" by Susan Kelleher

For my Professional Colleagues

For many pet care professionals and pet lovers, a career in assisting grieving pet parents has become a mission and passion. Pet funeral homes, pet loss operations, pet loss support services, and other services that help grieving pet parents have begun to emerge in many, many markets.

For those that are interested in starting a business to assist pet parents with the loss of their precious pets, myself and the Two Hearts Pet Loss Center team can generally be found making our way across the country to guide and consult with those that are wanting to bring meaningful pet death care services to their communities. From working with operations that want to add pet loss services to their existing business entity to guiding those that have been involved in pet death care with repositioning of their value offerings, we take great pride in being on the leading edge of these respectful services. Visit www.TwoHeartsPetLossCenter.com if you'd like to learn more about how to be a companion to grieving pet parents, how to start a pet loss business, or schedule pet loss and grief training courses for your team.

In our industry, we have been so blessed to have other professionals who have spent countless hours on educating others on pet loss services. Publications such as Kates-Boylston's *American Funeral Director, American Cemetery*, and *Funeral Service Insider* have been on the cutting edge of reporting on the benefits of a quality pet loss program. Furthermore, the caring team at the International Cemetery, Cremation and Funeral Association has also been instrumental in reporting on this incredible service through their publication, the *ICCFA Magazine*.

Learning Opportunities

As my passion for guiding grieving pet parents began to consume my life and become my life's mission, I found myself attending as many courses as I could relating to the area of death and grief. Of course the first place that I turned to further my education was at the Center for Loss in Fort Collins, Colo., and studying under my dear friend and mentor, Dr. Alan D. Wolfelt, founder of the Center for Loss. As I sat in his classes, ranging from children and grief to the study of hospice, I found myself constantly equating these grief studies to pets. As fate would have it with the first course that I attended, I learned that Dr. Wolfelt also had a love for pets. Therefore, it was a very natural addition for us to begin to teach the Pet Loss Companioning Courses at his sacred space, the Center for Loss. I was most proud to be the first recipient of the Death and Grief Studies Certification: Specialization in Pet Loss Companioning and then equally proud when he asked me to be the one to facilitate these valuable sessions!

My work continues to span the United States and Canada in educating others in the area of pet loss and grief, respectful death care services, as well as being a resource for grieving pet parents. For those areas that you need guidance and assistance, reach out to me. Let me help you, guide you, and, if applicable, honor your story.

AFTERWORD

My first pets, Snobal, Buddy, and Blackie – photo taken in 1982.

My Dear Pet Parent,

Thank you for taking a walk with me on this journey. I loved sharing these words with you. I hope the stories warmed your heart and that you found useful information to educate you in the area of pet loss, guidance in looking for a pet loss operation, and tidbits on how you can honor your precious pet.

You might have been a bit like me, touched to the point of tears with each story that I told, honoring these special pets. As I recalled the stories of Cherokee, Moet, Squirty, and the others that I had the honor of companioning, I too was brought to tears as I remembered all of the beautiful details of these families like it was yesterday. For each of these families, myself, and probably you too, it does seem like it was yesterday when we have experienced the loss of a beloved pet.

Weekly I'm on a plane, making my way to some destination where my work in this world of pet loss continues. Possibly it's consulting with someone on the start of their pet funeral home, speaking to a group of veterinarians or pet parents on pet loss, or educating others on the importance of a quality and meaningful pet loss program. As with many of us who fly, a conversation is generally started with a seat mate. My heart swells with the number of stories that I have heard of pets who have died, some recently and many times not so recently. But with each story, regardless of the time that has passed, invariably my seat mate sheds a tear. It amazes me that even on a plane full of hundreds of people, people are comfortable in recalling the life shared with a pet – and the love that was lost. But, bigger yet, it's the memories that are immediately recalled, the stories that flood back, and the unconditional love that for a brief moment of travel takes one back to a love that is missed. Each of these conversations invariably ends with the statement "I know others say it, but my dog was truly the best" or "I know you hear this a lot, but there wasn't another cat like mine." Yes, they were ***the best***.

I love honoring pets through their pet parents' stories. They are heartwarming and they are touching, full of learning of life's lessons and full of unconditional love. Yes, to honor them in death is to completely honor and respect the life that was lived.

I want to honor your story. My dear friend and colleague, Tom Parmalee, and I are compiling the second edition of our publication. Let us honor a furry love in your life. Email your story to me at Stories@TwoHeartsPetLossCenter.com and let us pay tribute to your beautiful life that was shared with a precious pet. After all, I do know that your pet was "the best ever."

Thanks for walking with me and letting me be a companion for you during your journey.

Warmly,

Coleen

ABOUT THE AUTHOR

Coleen Ellis opened up the first standalone pet funeral home in the United States, Pet Angel Memorial Center, in a strip mall in Indiana. A trailblazer in the world of pet funeral service, she's appeared on *Inside Edition* and has a weekly segment on a local television station near Greenwood, Ind., in conjunction with the Indianapolis Humane Society. Scores of articles and television spots focusing on her and her business have been distributed through local, regional, national and international media outlets.

After helping hundreds of pet parents celebrate and honor the lives of their pet children, she sold most of her stake in Pet Angel to a group of investors, but she still maintains a role and an ownership interest in the company. She now operates Two Hearts Pet Loss Center, a consulting firm that helps veterinarians and death-care and grief professionals serve clients affected by the death of a pet.

Ellis heads the Pet Loss Professionals Alliance, a subdivision of the International Cemetery, Cremation and Funeral Association, which is seeking to devise standards and best practices related to pet memorialization.

Ellis lives in Chicago, Ill. and Greenwood, Ind., with her husband, Chris Burke, and their furry children.

To learn more about the author, visit www.twoheartspetlosscenter.com.